W9-BWT-384

Creative
Fashion Design
with Illustrator®

Creative
Fashion Design
with Illustrator®

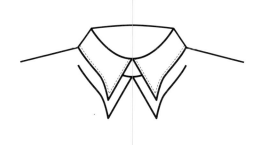

Kevin Tallon

BATSFORD

This book is dedicated to all those who helped me produce it, and all of those who will create great fashion design by using it. A special dedication goes to my partner Binia, who supported me through the countless long nights spent on writing and designing the content.

First published in the United Kingdom in 2006
by Batsford
151 Freston Road London W10 6TH

An imprint of Anova Books Company Ltd

Copyright © Batsford 2006

Text and pictures copyright © Kevin Tallon 2006

Adobe product screen shots reprinted with permission from Adobe Systems Incorporated.

Adobe Illustrator® is a registered trademark of Adobe Systems incorporated in the United States and other countries.

The moral right of the author has been asserted. All rights reserved. No part of this publication may be reproduced, stored in a retrieval system, or transmitted in any form or by any means electronic, mechanical, photocopying, recording or otherwise, without the prior written permission of the copyright owner.

ISBN 0 7134 9022 5
ISBN (13-digit) 9780 7134 9022 0

A CIP catalogue record for this book is available from the British Library.

10 9 8 7 6 5 4 3 2 1

Reproduction by Classicscan, Singapore
Printed and bound by WKT Co Ltd, China

This book can be ordered direct from the publisher at the website:
www.anovabooks.com

Or try your local bookshop

Contents

Introduction

What does creative fashion design with Illustrator mean? To answer this question, I need to go back to the time when the story starts: 1991, when I was in Geneva, Switzerland, running my own fashion label, creating designer wear for skateboarders. With no formal fashion training and driven solely by a need to materialize ideas for cool skate apparel, my days were essentially spent cutting locally bought fabrics into trousers and shorts. My evenings were spent riding and testing the shapes with my skater mates. One key element of my collections was T-shirts with bold logos and illustrations. Not short of creative energy, I would usually draw, photocopy, cut and paste graphics into some 'in your face' artwork, which was then manually printed with the help of friends.

About a decade earlier, I had been introduced to computers when a Sinclair ZX Spectrum landed in our flat. I was instantly hooked and spent hours loading games, by means of audiocassette, into the ridiculously slow but yet groundbreaking machine. Games offered a great way of getting used to the new computer interface. I felt that a 'special' relationship was growing between this small machine and me. Along with countless scores of youngsters across Europe, I became part of the first generation to discover home computing and gaming. The interactivity was great; remember that back then the PC did not even exist and the kind of machine we used had a memory of around 48K – less data than an average Jpeg picture!

A few years later came a key moment in my life. It was probably around the spring of '85 when, out of the blue, a good friend of mine introduced me to his brand new Apple Macintosh. He showed off by whizzing through the computer's features and capabilities, one of which totally threw me back: MacPaint.

MacPaint was one of the first graphics applications for the casual home user. The application was rudimentary, but totally groundbreaking. Basically, its interface created a template on which many creative media applications are still based. After about five minutes I could already spray-can funny shapes on the screen. It was really as simple as picking up a pen.

I came back from the weekend visit with only one thing on my mind: I needed to get my hands on an Apple Mac. The only snag was the price tag! Macs cost a small fortune back then and only graphic

MacPaint

design studios or rich individuals could afford them. I was neither. I would have to wait, a long time – a very long time.

Nearly ten years later, the idea of buying a Mac was a distant memory. I had discovered fashion design, frantically teaching myself pattern cutting and stitching. I was now into sewing machines big time, but a new encounter brought the little computer back on top of my agenda.

As I mentioned, T-shirts with prints were key to my collection and I was getting a little bored with the limited capabilities of hand-made print designs, which had an amateurish look and feel. Luckily, not far from where I lived, a friend of mine was running his own graphic design studio, complete with a few Apple Macs. We had to meet there! I arrived at his studio full of ideas, sketches and concepts. Subsequently, I spent a lot of time at the studio watching how my mate and his colleague worked on the Mac with Adobe Illustrator. Over time, something started growing inside me; I felt the strong urge to do exactly the same as they were doing – it looked so easy and fun. I had to get a Mac once and for all. Brand new was out of question, so I set my sights on a second-hand machine: a Mac colour classic with a whopping 40 MB hard drive and 10 MB of memory. I started working on Illustrator 3, which was already outdated back then, but still good enough as a tool on which to learn the basics of the application. Because the Mac was such an iconic piece of kit, it never felt like working on a computer, but more like working with a tool such as a pen or brush. This was later to become a key element of my methodology. I did not feel like becoming a slave to the computer and did not want to treat it differently from a brush. But of course it was millions of times superior to a brush and I treated it much better than my old unwashed paintbrushes!

The whole skate fashion scene was starting to bore me. Basically, once you had designed the perfect shorts, trousers and T-shirt, there was not much more you could create. I needed more challenge, more inspiration. I still did not have any formal fashion training and felt this was the opportunity to give it a go and broaden my knowledge. Again, it was by chance, after a discussion with a friend's mother, who happened to be a professional fashion designer, that I found out about Saint Martins School of Art. Without much reflection, I left everything behind and flew to London with one big bag containing my belongings and a huge box containing my Apple Mac and laser printer (to my father's exasperation, since he had to pay extra money on the spot for my outrageously overweight baggage).

Once in London, I applied for a summer course in fashion illustration. I loved drawing and was taught by my grandfather, who was a keen artist, creating neat cartoons and caricatures. Back in Geneva, I attended an evening course in life drawing and wanted to sharpen my skills with the added fashion design element. The course was run by Saint Martins and was my first step towards joining the famous art school. Six months later, I was formally applying to join the Fashion Menswear BA course. I was accepted and started the following autumn.

In my view, the key to the success of Saint Martins in producing highly creative individuals stems from the informal curriculum and nurturing environment of the school. I had a great time at the college and was able to give myself space and time to create new concepts and experiment with design ideas. Towards the end of my first year, I was offered a work placement at Katharine Hamnett during my summer break. The great thing was that I just happened to live next door to her studio. The second surprise was that Katherine had just

bought a brand new top-of-the-range Apple Power Mac 8100, with a huge 21-inch screen and a Fiery RIP (raster image processing), linked to a colour photocopier. This was the very best small office computer and printing system money could buy, but because it was brand new only a few people knew how to use it and pretty much no one knew how to use Illustrator. I had found my perfect match! At the end of my three-month work placement, I pleaded with the studio manager to keep me on because I could be useful as the one who could work on Illustrator and deliver some usable graphics, helping the Katharine Hamnett Denim designer. I was engaged on a free-lance basis, working in the studio two days a week while I was still studying. Over the next three years, I would learn how to work creatively on the Mac with Illustrator (and other applications) in a fashion design environment. This was when I started thinking about setting up my own business, based around graphics and fashion design. What was so exciting was the fact that all of this was brand new, like an unspoilt land full of promises and possibilities.

After leaving college, I had several clients for whom I started designing, with the added value of digital delivery. T-shirt graphics, flat drawings and trims were churned out merrily and delivered to satisfied clients. It was very important not to consider myself as a Mac operator, but rather as a creative designer, using the computer as a tool just like a pattern cutter or a textile designer. Crucially, I had to deliver the goods fast and neatly, so I could not afford to spend hours designing a single flat or print. This became a key element of my work: maximizing the work flow and productivity.

After three years of good and loyal services to various companies, ranging from the edgy East London urban brand to the mass-market High Street global company, I decided to launch my own label again. This gave me the freedom to design what I felt was appropriate. Quite often, when you work as a freelance designer or a consultant, you tend to work only on one specific part of the fashion business. By starting my own range again, I took on the challenge of learning all aspects of the business, from pricing to production issues and from sales to garment technology.

The challenge was daunting, but it helped to expand my range of skills on Illustrator, especially in terms of production design (size charts, spec sheets, modification sheets and so on). I started this new adventure with a business partner, who had the right set-up to distribute and produce the goods. I worked closely with factories and production agents in both Portugal and the UK, driven by the fact that, with the right factory or agent, you could design from the computer directly to a finished product, without the need for costly samples and prototypes. This newly emerging trend had a lot to do with the advent of the email availability to the masses, cheaper modems and service providers enabling users to send crystal-clear PDF (portable document format) and JPEG (bitmap image compression format) images. This was a far cry from the good old fax with its limited resolution and black-and-white colour range. From the mid '90s onwards, people started to discover the power of email, linked with the flexibility of these emerging new file compression formats.

It is interesting to note that since Illustrator works with vector graphics, a typical PDF version of a garment technical spec on an A4 sheet would not be bigger than 250K for a resolution of 300dpi. This meant that with the early 56k modems, Illustrator PDF files could be sent much faster than the equivalent quality JPEG. It suddenly became possible to send, at next to no cost, perfect technical drawings in full colour to a factory on the other side of the world in less than a few minutes. This, I believe, is one of the key factors, along with growing consumer demand and expectation, that explains why High Street outlets became able to produce up to 12 collections a year.

The pace suddenly became frantic. Long gone are the days when designers produced two collections a year. Because customers are today more interested in style than substance, they tend to replenish their wardrobe more often with cheap, throwaway items. Companies able to produce new, cheap and trendy garments every month are growing in influence and power. For my part, I realized that there was not much sense in carrying on competing when High Street garments were retailing at the price I normally would pay my factory. By the time I added my margin and the retailer his, the

garment was around five times more expensive than a High Street equivalent. My designs were more directional and unique, but for the average punter, this does not make it worthwhile unless, of course, the garment is produced by the type of big, well-known designer who can get away with selling a basic five-pocket pair of jeans for more than £200.

I eventually came back to freelance work and Saint Martins when Chris New, my menswear teacher, asked me to lecture for a project based on creating and delivering fashion design work on the computer. Chris felt that too many students still lacked the computer skills to meet the work market demands. Part of the project was allocated to hands-on workshops in a dedicated computer room. This is where I really started to develop a methodology based on how to teach Illustrator to fashion designers. This was a tough audience of highly individual creative minds, minds that usually had short attention spans for anything that involved sitting around and listening to 'how to do this or that' without being able to actually do anything. This informed another key aspect of the nascent methodology: there is nothing better than actually doing it yourself! I adapted my course over time and made it a more attractive offering for highly creative people wishing to design with a computer as easily and effortlessly as drawing with a pen, keeping in mind an element of fun and experimentation.

Over the next three years, I lectured on several fashion projects based on a similar format and started a computer evening class entitled 'Creative Fashion Design with Illustrator' with the help of the fashion course director, Willi Walters, and Chris New.

Over the past 15 years, I have developed skills and understanding based on the relationship between fashion, computer and creativity. This depth of knowledge and experience has given me the confidence to put forward a methodology and tutorials to help people work with Illustrator efficiently, creatively, professionally and, I hope, as easily as using a pen.

Chapter 1
The Methodology

The methodology has three main components: the tool (Illustrator and the computer); the user (their needs and aspirations), and the work (quality, creativity and delivery).

As you might have noticed in the introduction, I learned to use the tool by myself and devised over time a way of working with the application specifically for fashion. Bringing organic and adaptable growth into the application is the foundation of the methodology and rules over various aspects of it. For example, I will not bother learning what I do not need to know. Look at the official Illustrator user guide: it's over 400 pages long and that's without the tutorials. The guide simply explains in a linear fashion all the features of the application, without asking the user the key questions as to who he/she is and what he/she wants to do with Illustrator. The user is the second key theme in the methodology, which is first and foremost about people rather than empirical dogma. This book and its methodology are not about preaching the best and only way to work with Illustrator for fashion design. It's about listening to what kind of work people want to achieve with the application, giving them the opportunity to expand their creative skills working with this new and powerful tool and, most importantly, helping people to find the way the application works best for them. If Illustrator were a car, this book would help you go where you want, using the quickest and most efficient way.

The methodology's structure is primarily based on my computer course, which focuses on people, their needs and aspirations. Each person joining the course or reading the book will have their individual background and needs. The methodology attempts to cater for various demands and needs. Each tutorial is made into a self-contained format and can be removed or skipped if the reader feels it is irrelevant.

The methodology and tutorials should help readers to get a good start with Illustrator, making them confident enough to go beyond this book and explore new possibilities, adapting the application to their style.

People joining the course and learning the methodology have been so far either Saint Martins fashion students from different curriculums (women's and men's fashion design, knitwear design, fashion with marketing and fashion print design) or fashion

professionals seeking to learn Illustrator or broaden their skills. Because these people have different backgrounds and skills levels, they have different needs, so the methodology has been developed around this premise. It is therefore flexible and modular.

I observed in the introduction that creative people tend to want to get on with it and do things. Obviously, if they have come to the course, they want to learn, but I feel it is most important that the relationship between the methodology and people should never be top down. I want users to engage and seek help on how to do things, rather than be told what to do.

The kind of people that are more successful in mastering the tutorials and methodology are those who have a tendency to think laterally. Quite often, there is more than one way to do things and grasping this early on is essential. I have seen people with very little computer training, but the right kind of thinking, move rapidly forward. On the other hand, people who see the world in a linear fashion can get stuck too easily, not being able to go beyond hurdles because they feel that the only way forward is in a straight line rather than simply to walk around the problem.

A student shouldn't learn what is not necessary to him or her, but should rather focus on what is most important. Nevertheless a student should at least do two things:

- Learn the basics of the application relevant to fashion design
- Customize the tutorials for specific needs

For example, a pure fashion designer might want to learn how to make good fashion technical sketches, whereas a fashion print student will want to learn Illustrator painting and graphic tools. Both, however, will need to learn the basics if they want to be able to work on the tutorials that suit their needs.

Because of my creative background and Saint Martins' tendency to promote pure creativity and conceptual thinking, I like to help people develop their own style and promote new ways of creating design content. Once they have acquired the basics, they are left to their own devices to explore and discover the possibilities within the application. The tutorials are meant to be a compromise between different fashion levels and backgrounds. The flat drawings have the key ingredients inherent to their function, but do not go over the top in terms of details or styling. For example, a **jeans sketch** (right) will be a simple four-pocket style having all the elements commonly found on this type of design. Designers should want to go beyond the tutorial sketch and add their own design ideas and details, once they have mastered the basics of any particular design.

Another important aspect of the methodology is that one should learn how to draw freehand before working on a computer. Even in today's technology-driven world, nothing can yet replace the pen and paper. Computers have taken over the whole design production process of fashion, but it is still much faster to draw a quick sketch of any design idea on paper or in a sketchbook than to switch your computer on, launch Illustrator and finally start drawing a sketch. Certainly, some people use a stylus palette to draw freehand, but to be honest this is still neither good enough nor organic enough to be convincing. It is also important to research your project, coming up with as many inspirational images, clippings, drawings, details, colour inspirations, fabric swatches and so on as possible. This research will become important and help you create garments with more depth and background than before.

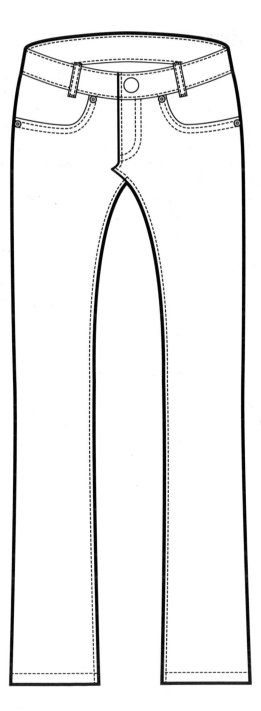

Standard four-pocket jeans

The tutorials

Beyond its theoretical aspect, the methodology in this book has a very practical approach and is entirely made up of tutorials. The content will start with simple and basic matters, evolving into advanced skills. Readers can therefore start with basics and must-know tutorials, before moving on to learning key Illustrator tools.

This is followed by a group of tutorials based on specific garment designs. Beyond this, the tutorials go into advanced skills, such as print and knitwear design. It is important to note that the more advanced the tutorial, the less obvious and repetitive steps will be included. In the earlier tutorials, the user will be able to follow every single step for any operation, whereas in the later ones the focus will be on more complicated or intricate issues. For example, in the earlier stage, if a duplication is mentioned, it will be written like this: *Duplicate shape* (right button press and drag shape then hold down the ALT key then release the mouse button), whereas beyond the basic tutorial, it will simply be *duplicate the shape*.

I encourage users to mix and match various tutorials to achieve a complete design. For example, a shirt sketch with a fabric stripe design and a placement print will need skills from three different tutorials Some tutorials contain Quick Tip sections, which will help users get an insight into some of the techniques used in the fashion industry to produce designs faster and more accurately.

Working with Illustrator

The methodology hinges on the premise that you can use an application such as Illustrator, which was not necessarily devised with fashion design in mind. So why not learn a fashion-centric design application? Because they tend to be expensive, hard to learn and can transform you into a 'Mac operator'. A Mac operator is someone who spends his time chained to a computer, doing non-creative production work for creative people. So Illustrator, in this respect, is a good choice, as it is relatively cheap and has a fairly shallow learning curve. This enables creative people to have a go at designing on the computer without feeling like geeks.

Because Illustrator is not a tailor-made fashion application, it can also do many things that other fashion-specific applications can't. Illustrator is a very powerful tool for any graphic design work you can throw at it. It is in many ways a jack of all trades, capable of doing a range of tasks, such as graphic design, fashion sketches, fashion illustration, trim design, fashion prints and so on. Illustrator is first and foremost a fashion design production tool. By fashion design production, I mean the work area, which sits between design research, including initial collection freehand sketch drawing, and final garment prototype, made by the factory. Basically, once you have created your collection freehand on paper, you can start developing it in Illustrator, producing more accurate flat drawings with all the front and back view details required. These will then be of a high enough standard to be sent straight to the factory to start prototypes production.

Always pushing the boundaries

Because the methodology was mainly devised in a creative learning environment, it has a strong experimental element within it. Many different needs can be catered for with a flexible application like Illustrator. The methodology's DNA is made to push the boundaries wherever possible. Within the methodology is embedded a true belief in experimentation and the drive to go beyond the norm.

To avoid a kind of creative anarchy, the methodology will start by looking only at essential features of specific tasks needed for fashion designers. Later on, the tutorials will evolve into more far-reaching features, such as Illustrator's symbols, brushes and styles. Once all tutorials are finished, the users should be confident enough to explore new possibilities and features, which might be developed in a new, exciting and unique way.

Another important element concerning the methodology and ever-renewed challenge is the desire to work faster and more efficiently as the methodology evolves, as Illustrator upgrades to new versions and as computers grow in power. Mirroring the demand for increased turnaround and fast-changing trends, a designer should be able to work faster by learning shortcuts, skills and tricks. I am always delighted to have a student show me a better, easier and faster way to do a mundane fashion design task (and there are a lot!), which will in turn enable them to 'buy' more time to work on the creative side of fashion design.

I hope this gives you a good understanding of what you are getting yourself into. One last thing to remember before you start: be patient and practise as much as you can; if you don't, you might forget everything you learned quite quickly. One final warning: don't forget to save your work before your computer crashes!

Chapter 2
Introduction to Illustrator

Adobe Illustrator was first developed for the Apple Macintosh in 1985. In those days, the Macintosh only had a monochrome 9in built-in display. Illustrator helped drive the development of larger monitors for the Macintosh because of the need for better definition in graphic and depth of colour. Illustrator 1.0 was quickly replaced by 1.1, which enjoyed widespread use. The next version (in a novel versioning scheme) was 88 (to match the year of release, 1988). This was followed by 3.0, which provided several useful features. Today, the latest version is Illustrator CS 2, also known as Illustrator 12. This book's tutorials have been created with both Illustrator 10 and Illustrator 12. Illustrator 12 has acquired several new features. We will use some of these new features in a few of the tutorials, clearly marked as Illustrator 12 features only. One such key feature is the new powerful Live Trace tool, which enables users to transform automatically a bitmap image into editable vectors. If, in this particular case, users do not work on Illustrator 12, there are other ways to get a similar result, which will be explained in the relevant tutorial. I recommend readers to work with at least Illustrator 10 in order to follow most of the tutorials with ease. Users with previous versions of Illustrator might miss out on the more advanced tutorials, which use functions such as brushes, gradient mesh and styles.

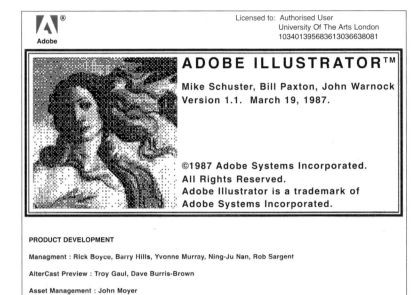

Illustrator 1.1

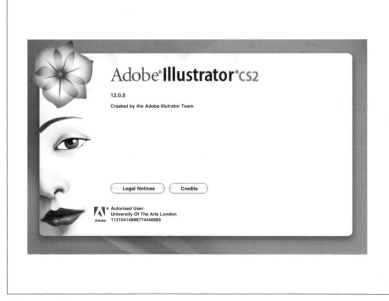

Illustrator CS2

Mac versus PC

This book and its tutorials are based on the Mac OS operating system (Mac OS X). To be fair, when using Illustrator, the difference between Mac and PC is small and usually remains in the keyboard shortcuts. PC users should simply follow the tutorials and in 99 per cent of cases use the Control key in conjunction with other keys rather than the Command key. Mac uses the Command key + various other keys for shortcut menu function (in other words, Command+O to open a document) whereas PCs uses the Control key + various other keys (Control+O to open a document). Quite often, on Mac platform, the Command key is referred to as the Apple key (it has an Apple logo on it). The GUI (Graphic User Interface) of both Mac OS X and Windows XP are very similar and any average computer user can make the transition from one to the other with little difficulty.

It is true that most computer users in the world today work on a Windows-based PC, so it seems strange to go for the Mac platform when wanting to reach the biggest audience possible. Three main factors make this thinking viable:

1. Illustrator was originally designed for the Mac (in 1985). It was only available for the PC in 1989 and only got a foothold on the PC market in 1995 with the PC version 4.1. PC users were mainly working with Corel Draw.

2. The Apple Mac GUI was developed in the early 80s and brought to the public in 1984 with the first Mac launch. This interface design, along with the mouse, was ground-breaking and set the standard for all personal computers. Even today, Windows XP and Mac OS X, as well as all major design applications, have striking similarities with the original Mac interface. Just take a look at MacPaint's tool palette, designed in the early 80s, and compare it to the Illustrator 12 palette or even the Photoshop palette. The point here is that it is much better to work with the original GUI rather than copies of it.

3. MacPaint and MacDraw applications launched the whole concept of an easy creative interface for computer users. As simple as using

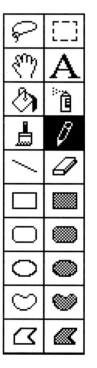
MacPaint
tool box

Illustrator CS2
tool box

a paintbrush or a spray can is what comes to mind when working on the MacDraw. Illustrator was designed around the MacDraw interface and, although over time it became much more powerful and feature rich, the simplicity of use and flexibility is still there to be seen and enjoyed. This 'creativity first' approach is crucial and is one of the key aspects of my methodology and teaching.

Regarding the age-old issue of the mouse design, it seems that finally Apple has come around and started selling a two-button mouse. This is great news. I personally opted for a third party two-button and wheel mouse long time ago. PC users are used to a multiple-button mouse and this book's tutorials are designed for a two-button mouse (the buttons are described here as the left or right button). For Mac users still working with a single-button mouse, simply press the Control key + mouse click to replace the right button click.

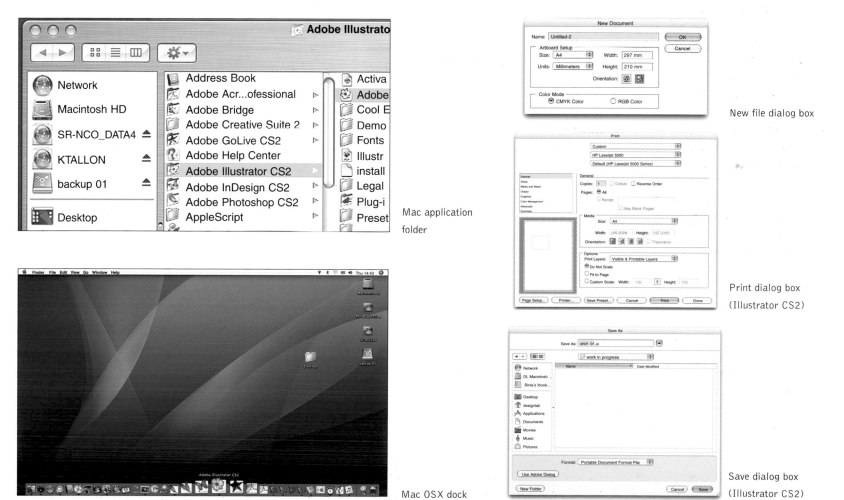

The application and your operating system

Like any other application, Illustrator works as a separate entity within your operating system. Usually, once you install the package onto your system, it will have its files automatically placed within the operating system. The application icon can be found inside the application folder in Mac and PC and the shortcut in the Start menu (PC) and Dock (Mac).

The interaction between Illustrator and the operating system is limited to three functions: opening files, saving and printing files.

I always strongly recommend students to save their files as often as possible. I have seen too many crashing computers and files with hours of work behind them lost forever. Make a habit of hitting Command+S (or Control+S for PC) whenever possible. I usually try to save every time I finish a key stage of my work. It is true that today computers tend to crash less than back in the old days, but still, better to be safe than sorry!

Mac application folder

New file dialog box

Print dialog box (Illustrator CS2)

Mac OSX dock

Save dialog box (Illustrator CS2)

Illustrator's interface

Illustrator has five main interface areas: the Command menu bar, the floating palettes, the artwork window, the dialog box and the context menu. Illustrator 12 has one extra interface area: the Control palette.

The **Command menu bar** gives you access to all the main functions of Illustrator and many of them can be reached with keyboard shortcuts.

The **floating palettes** are located on the right-hand side of the screen except for the **Tools palette**, which is on the left-hand side. Floating palettes can be accessed through the menu bar under Window. There are many different floating palettes. Quite a few are not useful for fashion design and it is better only to open the ones you really need and close those you don't.

All palettes have the following elements:

1. A title bar, which can be dragged to move the palette.
2. The palette window, which contains all the elements.
3. A tab with the palette name, which can be dragged and docked with other palettes.
4. A palette pop-up menu, which can be accessed by clicking on it.
5. Some palettes also have shortcut icons at the bottom of the window.

Illustrator CS2 interface

Command menu

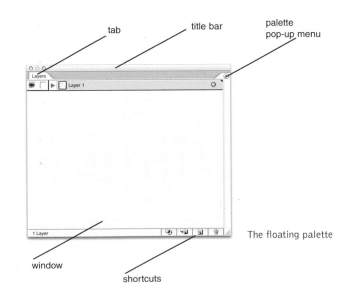

tab   title bar   palette pop-up menu

The floating palette

window

shortcuts

The **Artwork window** is where your canvas is located and where you will draw your artwork. Like many other graphic applications, the artwork window contains the following elements:

1. The title bar, which displays your file name and can be dragged to move your entire artwork window.
2. The canvas, which measures three metres square and displays your page at the centre.
3. The page, which represent your chosen paper size.
4. The page tiling, which shows the boundaries within which your printer will be able to print a single page.
5. The scroll bar, which enables you to scroll up and down and left and right.
6. The information tab, which displays information related to the tool you are using or the task you are performing.
7. The zoom display and pop-up menu, which displays the zoom value at which you are viewing your artwork.

The **Dialog box** appears when you need to enter values or make a choice for Illustrator to act upon. For example, when you create a new document, a dialog box appears in which you can choose the size of your page.

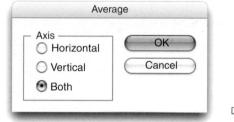

Dialog box

The **Context menu** is a shortcut to some of the Command menu bar functions. Illustrator contains a number of context-sensitive menus. Their content relates either to the object you have selected or to the document itself. You can access context menus by right click or Control click (if you work with a one-button mouse). Context menus are a much easier and faster way to access commonly used commands.

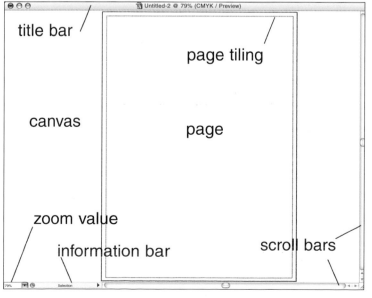

Artwork window

Context menu

The **Control palette** is a new Illustrator CS2 (12) feature and is related to the object you select on your artwork. The content and option of the control palette depends on what kind of object you select. For example, selecting a text object will show text formatting options in addition to basic options, such as colour and stroke. The control palette is a one-stop gap encompassing information that can be accessed and modified in other areas, such as the floating palettes and the Command menu bar.

Path	Fill:	Stroke: ■	1 pt	Opacity: 100	%	Style:	⊞	X: 44.45 mm	Y: 416.239	W: 323.85 mm	H: 189.089	

The way Illustrator works

Illustrator is a vector-based application, working with the Bézier curve, which is a parametric curve important in computer graphics. Vector graphics are made of lines and curves defined by mathematical objects called vectors. Vectors view graphics according to their geometric characteristics. On the other hand, a bitmap-based application, such as Adobe Photoshop, uses rows and columns of coloured pixels to define an object or picture. Take a red square, for example: in Photoshop it would be an equally defined amount of rows and columns of pixels. Illustrator, on the other hand, would work with a formula including three variables: width (x), height (y) and colour fill (red). What makes Illustrator so useful for fashion design is the fact that vector graphics are resolution-independent. This means you can make any object bigger or smaller without losing any definition, whereas an object created in Photoshop will start to look 'pixelated' if it is enlarged too much. Garment sketches created in Illustrator, at any size, can always be enlarged or shrunk and remain sharp and clear.

From version 9, Illustrator has been capable of handling bitmapped images, such as JPEG and Photoshop files, although the capabilities and performance are nothing to be compared with Photoshop. Nevertheless, this new feature is very useful for certain aspects of fashion design.

ILLUSTRATOR   PHOTOSHOP

Chapter 3
Basic Tutorials

In this chapter, you will learn how to get your first foothold into Illustrator and acquire the basic skills needed to work in this new environment. From beginner to advanced-user level, basic skills are essential and need to be mastered before anything else. Even at the highest design level, you will be using these skills constantly. Basic skills are not fashion-specific, but are essential for anyone wishing to use the application. The basic skills can be divided into three main topics:

1. Working with the interface
2. Object manipulation
3. Viewing and navigating

A tutorial will be dedicated to each of these topics, but first let's look at how to get started with Illustrator.

BASIC TUTORIAL 1

Getting started

Usually, when you get into a new car you check your seat position, adjust the rear-view mirror and make yourself comfortable before hitting the road; you should do the same with any new computer application. In this case, you will need to set up Illustrator to suit a fashion designer's needs.

Input devices

The keyboard

Illustrator, like many other applications, uses a plethora of keyboard shortcuts to access its menu commands. Usually, more advanced users of the software tend to use keyboard shortcuts more, because they enable you to work much faster. In my own classes, I invite users to learn the most commonly used keyboard shortcuts at a gradual pace.

For the time being, all you need to know is that when you read through the tutorials in this book, keyboard shortcuts will be written in brackets, as follows: open the file (Command+O) Mac OS or (Control+O) Windows. To make a keyboard shortcut work, you just need to press the two keys simultaneously for a short while until you see the open dialog box or any other interaction on your screen.

The mouse

The mouse is your main input device and will be used extensively. It is important at this stage to understand the different mouse actions that you will need to differentiate in order to progress in the tutorials. There are four main mouse actions to learn and recognize in the tutorials:

Single click (left or right button): this is the most basic action, in which you point your mouse to the desired area, be it an object, a tool or Command menu, and swiftly single click the desired mouse button. It is important to note that in the tutorials a single click with the left button will always be referred as 'single click', whereas a single click with the right button will be referred as 'single right click'. This is because the majority of single clicks are with the left button.

Double click: as above, but with a double swift click and only with the left button.

Press and drag: for this action, press the left mouse button and keep it pressed down as you drag the mouse in any direction. This action is used to move objects, area-select objects and create Bezier curves.

Click away: this enables you to rapidly deselect one or many objects on your page. To click away, single click on any blank space on the art board.

When you **first launch Illustrator**, you will see the following: either an interactive window asking you to choose which kind of document you want to open (Illustrator 11 and 12) or simply the Tool palette and a preset number of floating palettes on the right-hand side (Illustrator 10 and below.) For Illustrator 11 and 12 users, simply select an A4 portrait document and press Enter on the keyboard or the OK button. For other Illustrator users, press Command+N (or Control+N Windows) or Menu >File>New to create a new document, and then select the same (A4 portrait) and press OK or Enter on the keyboard.

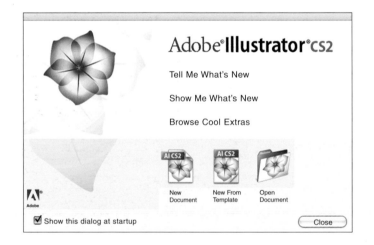

In the new document dialog box, you can choose either RGB mode or CMYK mode. Usually RGB (red, green, blue) is for screen-based graphics and CMYK (cyan, magenta, yellow, black) is for print work. Tick CMYK.

Document window

The document window contains the canvas on which you will create your artwork. In the centre is the A4 portrait page you just created and the printable area (dotted line), the size of which varies depending on your printer type. Basically, anything that is not within the printable area will not print out. In the lower left corner you can see the information tab, which usually displays the selected tool (by default the black arrow aka Selection tool).

Next to it is the zoom display window. By default, the zoom value is set to Fit in Window view, meaning that your A4 page will fit perfectly on the artwork window. Depending on your screen size, the percentage can change. I personally seldom use this window and prefer to use keyboard shortcuts to zoom in or out.

Floating palettes

Depending on your screen size and resolution, your artwork view can be covered by too many floating palettes. When you start working with Illustrator, having too many palettes can be confusing and slow your workflow as you try to find the right palette. It is useful to only open the palette you need to use to begin with. As the tutorials progress, we will open required palettes. Remember that palettes are tabbed and quite often you will find different palettes in the same window. Some of these you will need and some you won't. If you don't need a palette, simply press and drag the unwanted palette tab out of the group, and then single click on the red dot (or cross for Windows) to delete it.

Because different readers might be using different versions of Illustrator and these different versions might have different palettes open at start up, we will delete every floating palette displayed (apart from the tool box). To do this, single click on the red dot (or cross for Windows users) of each palette window. Once this is done, go to Menu>Window and select the following palettes: **Align**, **Swatches**, **Colour**, **Layer** and **Stroke**. When you select a listed floating palette, they might come grouped in a single window with other unwanted palettes. You can either drag out the unwanted palettes and delete them or leave them in place, as explained above. Your work area should now look like this:

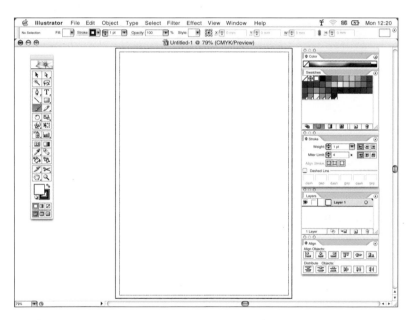

Tools palette

One of the most important floating palettes is the **Tools palette** (or Toolbox), to be found on the left-hand side of your screen. The tools are arranged over two columns and 13 rows, making a total of 26 tools. Actually, there are many more tools than this! Illustrator has tools embedded within certain tools; this is visualized by the little triangle symbol found in the lower right corner of some tool icons.

Some embedded tools will be needed more than others over the course of the tutorials. To access the embedded tools faster, you can 'tear off' the embedded tools, which then become their own separate floating tool palette.

To tear off an embedded tool, do the following:

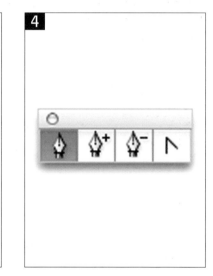

tear off

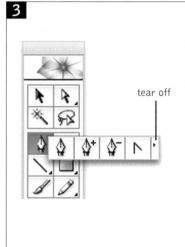

1 Point your mouse cursor on the pen tool icon.

2 Press with left mouse button for a while until you see the embedded pen tool palette.

3 Move towards the right of the embedded palette, keeping your mouse button pressed, and go right to the end of the palette where the tear off tab is located.

4 Once over the tear off tab, release your mouse button. This will release the palette from the main tool palette. You can move the floating palette to a more convenient location by dragging the palette top bar.

Preferences

Numerous programme settings are managed by Illustrator's preferences, covering various aspects of the application. We only need to change or check a few preferences to begin with:

6

Preferences

| General | ▲▼ |

Keyboard Increment: 0.3528
Constrain Angle: 0
Corner Radius: 4.23mm

OK
Cancel
Previous
Next

☐ Object Selection by Path Only ☐ Disable Auto Add /Delete
☐ Use Precise Cursors   ☐ Use Japanese Crop Marks
☑ Show Tool Tips   ☐ Transform Pattern Tiles
☑ Anti–aliased Artwork   ☐ Scale Strokes & Effects
☐ Select Same Tint %   ☐ Use Preview Bounds
☑ Append [Converted] Upon Opening Legacy Files

Reset All Warning Dialogs

5 Go to Menu>Illustrator>Preferences>General (Command+K or Control+K for Windows).

6 In the preferences dialog box, make sure that Scale Strokes & Effects and Transform Pattern Tiles are ticked.

7 Single click the pop-up menu (top left, where General is written) and select Units & Undo; in the Units menu, under General, select millimetre.

8 Press OK to confirm.

Scale Strokes & Effects means that when you scale any object up or down the stroke value will grow or shrink accordingly. Transform Pattern Tiles means that when you rotate an object with pattern tiles, the pattern will follow the rotation angle (see chapter 11 on how to create pattern tiles).

BASIC TUTORIAL 2

Views and navigation

Before you design anything in Illustrator, you should learn how to view any object on your A4 sheet and navigate within the canvas. Since you need something to look at, you will start by drawing a couple of very simple shapes and then experiment with different views and navigation techniques.

1

3

1 In the Tool palette, select the Square tool by single clicking it. Move your mouse back to the centre left of the A4 sheet.

2 Press and drag your mouse toward the lower right; a square should appear, and when you are happy with its size, release the mouse button.

3 Repeat the same operation from step 2 only. This time, start from the centre right of the A4 sheet. Your artwork should look something like the picture.

Now that you have two square objects to look at, located in two different places on your page, you can start using several viewing modes.

Viewing modes

Illustrator has two viewing modes: Preview and Outline. By default, you will always work in **Preview** mode, which shows you all the objects you have created in full colour, just as they would appear if you were to print them out. The **Outline** mode is not dissimilar to a wireframe view, where all object segments are displayed as very thin black lines, without any colour or stroke weight. The outline viewing mode is very useful when you have complex shapes, with segments close to one another. Outline allows you to be more precise when selecting segments or anchor points. To change viewing mode, do the following:

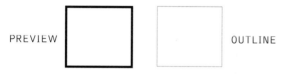

PREVIEW   OUTLINE

4 Go to Menu>View>Outline to see in outline view or press Command+Y (Control+Y for Windows).

5 To return to Preview mode, go to Menu>View>Preview or press Command+Y.

Zooming

You can easily zoom in and out of your canvas with Illustrator, from 3 per cent up to 6400 per cent. To zoom in and out, do the following:

6 In the Tool palette, select the Zoom tool by single clicking it. Move your mouse back towards one of the squares and single click on it; repeat this until the square fills your screen.

7 To zoom back out, simply press the Alt key while you single click the mouse button.

■ **Quick tip**

You should always position the Zoom tool in the centre of the object you want to zoom in or out of, and do this at every step, just like aiming and shooting at moving targets.

Quite often, when zooming into an object, you will need to click several times before you get the desired view. There is a faster way of doing this:

With the zoom tool selected, position the cursor towards the top-left corner, slightly outside the square you want to zoom into.
Press and drag towards the bottom right; you will see an area selection frame growing from your starting point.
Make the selection frame as big as you need and what is inside the frame will zoom in to fit your art board window.
Release the mouse button to confirm the zoom area.

You can use the area selection frame technique (see tip) to zoom into objects, but not to zoom out, since you would need to draw a selection frame that lay beyond what you see in your art board window.

View menu

The view menu contains several useful viewing modes, which can be used on a regular basis and are quite often more appropriate than the Zoom tool. To use different viewing modes, do the following:

8 Go to Menu>View> Fit in Window (Command+0 [zero] or Control+0 for Windows). Your A4 page will fit neatly in the art board window.

9 If you want to view your artwork in actual size, go to Menu>View>Actual Size (Command+1 or Control+1 for Windows).

■ **Quick tip**

You can also use the keyboard shortcut Command+ to zoom in or Command– to zoom out. This is faster and more convenient than swapping your current tool for the Zoom tool.

Navigation

Navigating enables you to go from one object to another. This is useful when you work in close-up views, which create longer distances from one object to the other. There are several different ways of navigating, as described below.

The scroll bar

This is the least precise navigation tool, and can result in you being lost on the art board, especially when you are close up to any object. To use the scroll bar, do any of the following:

10 With the mouse, point toward the vertical or horizontal scroll bar cursors and, once above it, press and drag up or down. Your page will shift upwards or downwards accordingly.

11 You can also use the scroll arrows located at the bottom of your vertical scroll bar and on the right-hand side of the horizontal scroll bar. Simply single click repeatedly on one arrow or the other to navigate to the required location.

The Navigator palette

The navigator palette is a small-scale representation of your art board window. The navigator palette can both zoom in and out and navigate through your art board. To use the palette do as follows:

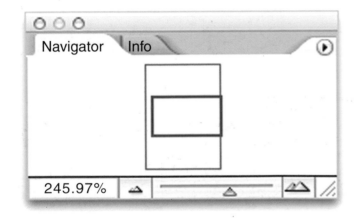

12 Go to Menu>Window>Navigator. Bring your mouse cursor over the navigator palette.

13 Press and drag the slider bar left to zoom out and right to zoom in.

14 Navigate your art board by pressing and dragging inside the navigator window. When you hover above this window with your mouse, the pointer will change into a hand cursor.

The Hand tool

The Hand tool is found in the toolbox and works in the same way as moving a real piece of paper with your hand. The Hand tool is useful for short distance movements, when you need to move the page slightly in order to have a better view of any object you are working on.

When used with its keyboard shortcut, the Hand tool becomes the fastest way to move around. To use the Hand tool, do the following:

Select the Hand tool in the toolbox.
Bring it over the page.
Press and drag to move the page around.
Release your mouse when you are happy with the new position.

■ Quick tip

The fastest way to both navigate and zoom is to use the keyboard shortcuts. As these are all located in the same area of the keyboard, this makes them very handy and fast to use:

To move your page around with the Hand tool, press the space bar and keep it pressed while you press and drag the mouse.
To zoom in, press the space bar and the Command key (Control for PC) while either single clicking or pressing and dragging the mouse.
To zoom out, press the space bar+Command+Alt (Control+Alt for PC) while single clicking the mouse.

BASIC TUTORIAL 3

Simple Object Creation and Manipulation

Illustrator has ready-made shapes, which are best suited to create your first objects. It's much better to start with these simple pre-designed shapes, since at this point the focus is on manipulation rather than the creation of custom-made objects, such as garment flats. The Rectangle tool is the most obvious ready-made shape and embedded within it are other shape tools, such as the Round-corner rectangle, the Ellipse, the Star and the Polygon.

We will work with some of these pre-designed shapes over this tutorial.

To create any of these shapes, do the following:

1   Create a new A4 portrait document: Menu>File>New or Command+N (Control+N for Windows).

2   Tear off the embedded shape tool palette and place it in a convenient place (see Basic tutorial 1 on how to do this).

3   Select the Ellipse tool by single clicking it.

4   Bring your mouse cursor back to the middle of your page; press and drag the mouse. You should see an ellipse appearing.

5   Release the mouse button.

I invite you to create as many different objects on your page as possible, using the various shape tools in order to experiment with them.

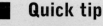

■ Quick tip

Do not use the Flare tool, as this tool is not a shape tool, but a lens flare effect simulation.

You can also create objects using the Shape tool dialog box. This enables you to enter precise object dimensions before they appear on the page.

To create objects using the dialog box, do as follows:

6   Select the Round Corner Rectangle tool by single clicking it.

7   Point your mouse cursor back to your page where you want to locate this new shape and single click the mouse.

8   In the dialog box, enter values for the width, height and corner radius.

9   Press OK to confirm.

8

Rounded Rectangle

Options
Width: 35.2778
Height: 35.2778
Corner Radius: 4.2333 mm
OK
Cancel

Object selection

When you create more than one object in Illustrator, the application keeps only the last created object selected. If you want to manipulate any other object, you will need to select it first. There are several ways in which you can select and deselect objects.

To select any single object:

10   Pick the direct selection tool (black arrow).

11   Single click the object's outline edge.

12   Your object is selected when a bounding box appears around it.

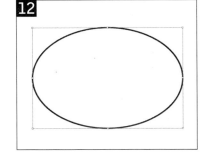

To multiple select any objects:

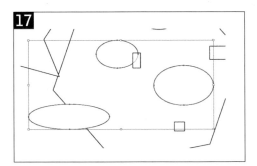

13   Using the black arrow, start by clicking on the first object you want to select.

14   Move towards your next object and, before selecting it, press the Shift key.

15   Move to your third object and click on it.

16 Keep the Shift key pressed until you have selected all the objects you want.

17 Release the Shift key.

To area-select any objects:

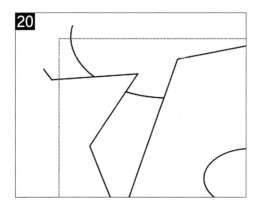

18 Using the black arrow, move toward the top-left corner and slightly outside the area bounding the group of objects you want to select.

19 Press and drag towards the bottom right; this will create an area selection frame.

20 When your area select frame covers the group of objects you want to select, release the mouse button.

The area-selection technique is fast but not very precise. A much more precise way of area selecting is to use the **Lasso tool**.

This only came to Illustrator from version 10 onwards, coming directly from Photoshop, but it has now become an indispensable tool with which to select objects. It is very useful when your selection area cannot fit into a rectangle.

To lasso select any objects:

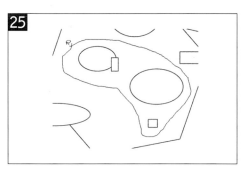

21 Select the Lasso tool in the Tool palette (Illustrator 10 users need to access it via the embedded tool).

22 Go towards the objects you want to select, but slightly outside.

23 Press and drag your mouse around the objects you want to select.

24 Finish by coming back to where you started, completing the loop.

25 Release the mouse button.

You can easily select all the objects on your art board.

To select all objects:

either go to Menu>Select>All
or Command+A (Control+A Windows).

■ Quick tip

Illustrator 10 users have two Lasso tools, a black one (to select entire objects) and a white one (to select part of an object), while Illustrator CS users only have one white lasso. If you are working with version 10, use the black lasso; if you are working with CS and CS2, to select an entire object, make sure you go around it fully without touching it.

Deselection and deletion

You might want to **deselect** some or all the objects you have selected previously.

26   Single click with the black arrow any object which is already selected, while pressing Shift.

27   Click away with the black arrow (if you have many objects selected, this will deselect them all).

28   Go to Menu>Select>Deselect or Command+Shift+A (Control+Shift+A for Windows)

To delete single unwanted objects do the following:

29   Pick the Direct Selection tool (black arrow).

30   Click anywhere on the edge (black stroke) of the object you wish to delete.

31   When the bounding box appears, press the Backspace key (located towards the top-right corner of keyboard) or the Delete key.

32   You can also go to Menu>Edit>Clear.

To delete all objects on your art board, do either of the following:

33   With the black arrow, go towards the top-left corner of your art board, making sure you can see all the objects you created. (Zoom out if necessary.)

34   Press and drag towards the bottom-right of your art board. When your selection area frame contains all objects, release the mouse button.

35   Press Backspace or Delete on the keyboard.

36   Go to Menu>Select>All or Command+A (Control+A Windows). Press Delete or Backspace on the keyboard.

You might not have wanted to delete all your objects or made mistakes when creating your objects, Illustrator can easily step back in time and then forward again if necessary. This is called simply Undo and Redo.

To undo a step, do the following:

37   Press Command+Z (Control+Z Windows) or Menu>Edit>Undo to go back one step.

38   You should now see all your objects again.

39   Press Command+Z again and repeat it as many time as needed until you have no more shapes on your art board.

To redo a step, do the following:

40   Press Command+Shift+Z (Control+Shift+Z for Windows) or Menu>Edit>Redo.

41   Repeat this until you come back to the artwork containing all the objects.

Now that all your objects are back on the art board, you should save your file.

■ **Quick tip**

You can only undo and redo when the file is open. Once it's closed, you cannot open it again and undo any mistakes made in previous sessions.

Saving your artwork:

42

Save As

Save As: artwork 1.ai

◄ ► ≣ ▥   📁 artworks

Network
DL Macintosh HD
Binia's lbook s...
Desktop
designlab
Applications
Documents
Movies
Music
Pictures

Name   ▲   Date Modified

Format: Portable Document Format File

Use Adobe Dialog

New Folder   Cancel   Save

42 Go to Menu>File>Save or Command+S (Control+S Windows).

43 In the Dialog box, name your file, and then select the folder in which you want to save your file or create a new folder by clicking on the new folder button located in the lower-left corner of the dialog box. By default, Illustrator chooses the Ai file format (Illustrator 12 PDF/Ai format), which is fine.

44 Press OK.

You can also save different versions of the same file:

45 Go to Menu>File>Save As or Command+Shift+S (Control+Shift+S Windows).

46 In the dialog box, give your file a new name or the same name with a version number. Select the folder in which you want to save your file or create a new folder by clicking on the new folder button.

47 Press OK.

Your file is now saved, and you can close the document window with Command+W (Control+W Windows) or Menu>File>Close. You can also click on the red button on the top-left corner (or X button, top right, for Windows)

Object manipulation

Having created, selected and deleted various objects, the next logical step is to perform different kinds of manipulation on them. Illustrator uses a bounding box when an object is selected, as you have seen before. Various manipulation features are embedded within the bounding box: rotate, corner scale, horizontal scale and vertical scale.

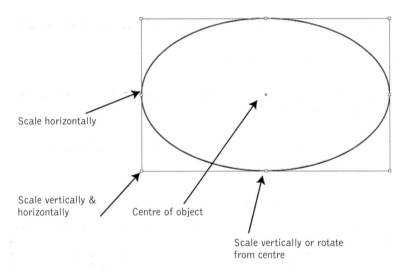

Scale horizontally

Scale vertically & horizontally

Centre of object

Scale vertically or rotate from centre

For this tutorial, we will draw a simple ellipse. It is important to note that any selected objects works under the same principles. So what you are learning now with a simple ellipse will be exactly the same for any garment sketches. Let's start by creating a new document and drawing an ellipse onto it:

48 Go to Menu>File>New or Command+N (or Control+N Windows).

49 In your Object floating palette select the Ellipse tool.

50 Press and drag on your page to create an ellipse.

To resize your object do as follows:

51 Select the black arrow.

52 Go over the ellipse shape, which should already be selected (if not, click anywhere on its black stroke).

53 Point towards the top-left corner of the bounding box, right on top of it; the arrow cursor will change into this symbol:

54 When the symbol is showing, press and drag the mouse either towards the centre of the ellipse or away from the centre.

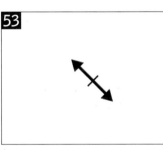

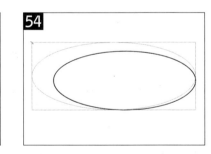

To resize your object only vertically or horizontally, do as follows:

55 With the black arrow, go over the bounding box, either on the top or bottom middle edge or on the left or right middle edge.

56 Your arrow should change either into the symbol on the left for vertical scaling (centre top or centre bottom edge of bounding box), or to the symbol on the right for horizontal scaling (centre left or centre right edge of bounding box).

57 Press and drag the mouse towards the left (the right for horizontal scaling) or towards the top or bottom for vertical scrolling (see both the illustrations).

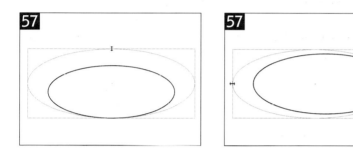

To rotate any objects, do as follows:

58 Proceed exactly as you have done when resizing the ellipse. Select the black arrow and with it select the ellipse, if it is not yet selected.

59 Go towards the top-left corner, but this time, slightly outside the bounding box, you should see your arrow changing into the side rotation symbol.

60 Press and drag the mouse towards the top right or bottom left (in a circular motion), to rotate the ellipse.

61 Release the mouse to confirm the rotation angle.

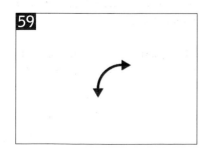

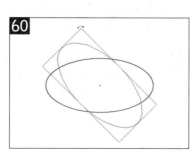

Using the scale and rotate tools

If you want more precision, the scale and rotate tools are better than the bounding box for simple scale and rotate operations. They both have dialog boxes to input rotation or scale values and work with a movable target, from which the rotation or scale is based.

To use the scale or rotate tools, do either of the following:

61 Select with the black arrow the object you want to rotate or scale.

62 Select the Rotate or Scale tool.

63 If you want to move the scale or rotation target, just press and drag it to a new position.

64 Press and drag in a circular motion (Rotate tool) or at an angle (Scale tool).

65 Release the mouse button.

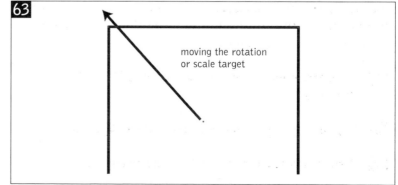

moving the rotation or scale target

For more precision:

66 Select with the black arrow the object you want to rotate or scale.

67 Double click the Rotate or Scale tool.

68 In the dialog box input the scale or rotate value.

69 Press OK to confirm.

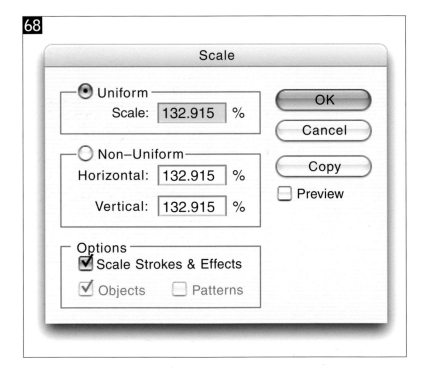

You are now able to create, delete, scale and rotate pre-designed objects. The next step is to look at how to move, duplicate and constrain them.

Moving objects

To move any objects, do as follows:

70 With the black arrow, select your ellipse.

71 Press and drag the outer edge of the ellipse (anywhere on the ellipse).

72 Move the ellipse to wherever takes your fancy.

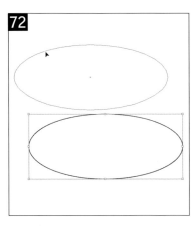

73 Release the mouse button.

You can also move an object, using the keyboard arrow keys (usually located between the main keyboard and numeric pad).

To use the arrow keys to move an object, simply do the following:

74 Select your object with the black arrow.

75 Press on any arrow key several times to make your object move towards your chosen direction.

■ **Quick tip**

You can keep the arrow key pressed continuously until your object has moved to where you want it. You can also set up the arrow key increment value in Menu>Illustrator>Preference>General and, in the keyboard increment box, type in the value you want. You can, for example, give a small value, if you want to have precise movement, or give big values to move an object swiftly across your art board.

Duplicating

To duplicate an object, do the following:

76 Select your object with the black arrow.

77 Press and drag it to a new position.

78 Before you release the mouse button, press the Alt key.

79 Release the **mouse button first**, and then release the Alt key.

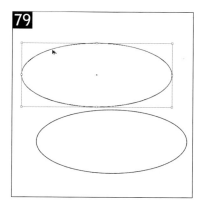

■ Quick tip

Any duplication action you make can be repeated automatically (both the distance and angle of duplication). After having duplicated your object, press Command+D (or Control+D for Windows) as many times as you need to duplicate your object again and again.

Constraining

Constraining restricts any actions, such as scaling, moving or duplicating, to certain parameters. For example, if you move an object horizontally, and constrain your movement at the same time, your object will slide in a perfectly straight line. Usually, to constrain you will need to press the Shift key while you are scaling, rotating or moving an object. However, because Shift can be used to select multiple objects as well, it is important in this case to press the Shift key only after you have started the motion you want to have constrained (scaling, moving, rotating and so on). All the manipulations you have learned previously can have a constraining action applied, let's quickly scan through them:

Scale constrain: press Shift after you have started to scale your object, which will then be constrained to resize proportionally only (this is very useful when resizing garment sketches, as it makes sure they are kept in proportion).

Rotate constrain: Press Shift after you start rotating your object, which be locked into 45-, 90-, 135- and 180-degree angles (useful, again, for many fashion applications, including bias cut lines or mirroring).

Move constrain: Press the Shift key after you start moving an object. It will snap and slide on an invisible line, either at 45 or 90 degrees (depending on the direction in which you are moving your object).

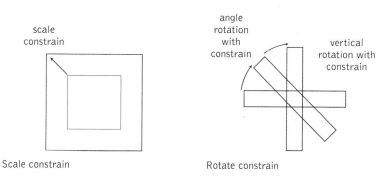

Scale constrain

Rotate constrain

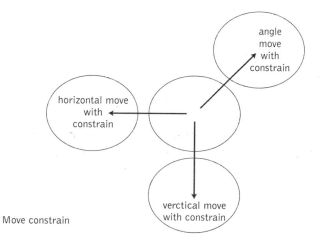

Move constrain

Duplicate and constrain

You can both duplicate and constrain any object at the same time. But you cannot duplicate and constrain an object when scaling or rotating, using the bounding box. You need to use the Scale and Rotate tools.

To duplicate and constrain move:

80   Select your object with the black arrow.

81   First move your object in any direction, and then press the Shift and Alt keys.

82   Release the mouse button then both keys.

To duplicate and constrain scale:

83   Select your object with the black arrow.

84   Select the Scale tool.

85   Scale your object first, and then press the Alt and Shift keys.

86   Release the mouse button to confirm the scaling then both keys.

To duplicate and constrain rotate:

87   Select your object with the black arrow.

88   Select the Rotate tool.

89   Scale your object first then press the Alt and Shift keys.

90   Release the mouse button to confirm the scaling then both keys.

You now have learned all the basic functions that you require to create and manipulate simple pre-designed shapes. Let's put these new skills to good use: in other words, let's put what you have learned into some fashion action!

91   With the Rectangle tool, create a small (3cm) square in the top-left corner of your A4 sheet. (Remember to press Shift to constrain the rectangle into a square.)

92   Select the black arrow and press and drag the lower edge of your square, directly below its original position. At the same time, press Shift to constrain your movement vertically and Alt to duplicate your square.

93   Release the mouse button and then the Shift and Alt keys when you have moved the square about 5cm below the starting position.

94   You should now see two squares perfectly aligned on a vertical axis.

95   Repeat your last action by pressing Command+D (Control+D Windows). This will automatically copy the moving distance and angle from your last action.

96   You should now see three squares.

97   Repeat again, pressing Command +D twice. You should now have five squares, equidistant from each other.

98   If your last square lands outside your A4 sheet, delete all the squares except the first one, then start again from step 2, but with a shorter distance between the squares.

This is as much as we can do for now with what you have learned so far. Save the file (Command+S) and name it 'five squares'.

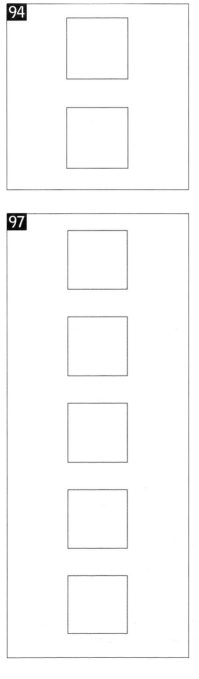

BASIC TUTORIAL 4

Selection tools, the white arrow

The white arrow (Direct Selection tool), unlike the black arrow, enables you to directly select anchor points and segments of any given object. This is useful when, for example, you need to retouch parts of a garment shape.

To modify objects with the white arrow, do the following:

1 Create a new document.

2 Select the Polygon tool.

3 Press and drag, then hold down the Shift key to constrain.

4 Release the mouse button.

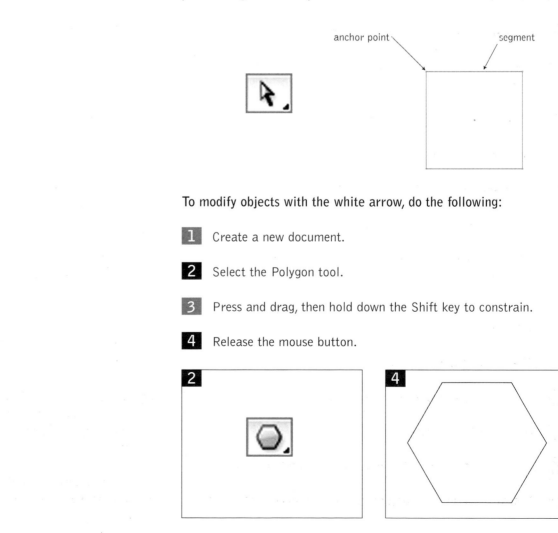

 Select the white arrow.

6 Click away.

7 Point your mouse directly above one of the polygon's segments.

8 Press and drag the segment to a new position.

9 Repeat the last action on another segment.

10 Play around and modify more segments to create a totally new shape.

Moving an object's segments to create an almost unrecognizable new one is only the first step: you can alter an object even further by directly moving the anchor points.

11 With the white arrow, go directly over any anchor point; the arrow icon should have a small square added to its side.

12 Press and drag the anchor point in any direction you wish.

13 Repeat the action with other anchor points.

14 Play around to transform your object into something totally new.

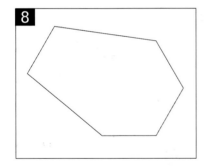

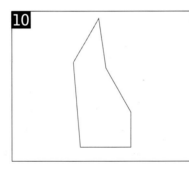

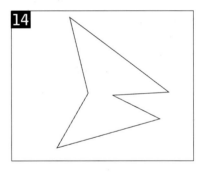

■ Quick tip

You can also select multiple anchor points with the white arrow, either by clicking them one by one while pressing the Shift key, or by area selection (press and drag over them). You can also use the Lasso tool (white lasso for Illustrator 10) by 'lassoing' the anchor points you want to modify.

BASIC TUTORIAL 5

Colour essentials

From the first tutorial onwards, all the objects you have created have had a white fill and a black stroke. This is because Illustrator, by default, applies these two colours to any new object created and they will remain this way unless the user changes the colours. The **Fill and Stroke squares** found in the Tool palette represent your selected object's colour status, the fill square representing the fill colour and the stroke square (with a hole in the middle) the stroke colour. When an object is selected, you can directly change its colour status by using these two squares as an interface in various ways. By default, the fill square is on top of the stroke square, but just as with playing cards, the lower square can be shuffled on top by clicking on it. The square in the foreground will be the one you can apply a new colour to, so remember that before you change an object's fill or stroke you will have to make sure that the fill or stroke square is on top and fully visible.

Fill square   Swap Fill & Stroke

Default Fill & Stroke   Stroke square

To apply colour to any object:

1 Open your 'five squares' document, created in Basic Tutorial 3; Command+O (Control+O for Windows) or Menu>File>Open.

2 With the black arrow, select the top rectangle.

3 Look at the fill square in the Tool palette and check that it is on top.

4 If it isn't, single click on it.

5 Go to the Swatch palette and select any colour that takes your fancy by single clicking on it.

6 Your fill square should now contain the new selected colour.

7 Go back to the toolbox and single click the stroke square to bring it to the front.

8 Go back to the Swatch palette and select another colour, making sure it's different from the first one you chose.

9 Your square should now have a new stroke colour.

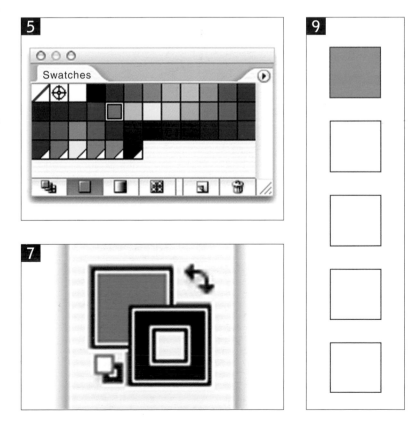

To swap the stroke and fill colours:

10 With the black arrow, select the top square.

11 In the Tool palette, click on the double-sided arrow icon next to the fill and stroke squares.

12 If you click on the double-sided arrow again, it will swap the colours back to what they were originally.

An object can also have no fill or no stroke applied to it, but to actually see this you will need to switch on the transparency grid, since Illustrator uses white as a background colour.

To apply no fill or no stroke colours:

13 Go to Menu>View>Show Transparency Grid or Command+Shift+D (Control+Shift+D for Windows).

14 Select the second square with the black arrow.

15 Make sure the stroke square is on top.

16 Go to the Swatch palette and select the no fill swatch or go to the no fill swatch in the tool box.

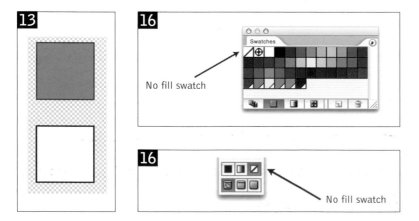

13

16
No fill swatch

16
No fill swatch

You might want to turn the transparency grid off again. To do so, go to Menu>View>Hide Transparency Grid or Command+Shift+D (Control+Shift+D for Windows). If you now click away or press Command+Shift+A (or Control+Shift+A Windows), your square will become totally invisible, since it is white on a white background. You can easily guesstimate where it is by comparing its position in relation to the other squares. Select it again with the black arrow or, if you cannot locate it, turn the transparency grid on again and then select the square.

Make sure that your fill square is on top in the Tool palette; if it is not, click on it. Go to the Swatch palette and choose a colour to replace the white fill. Save your document.

■ **Quick tip**

You can also use the default Fill & Stroke shortcut (black stroke and white fill) in the Tool palette to quickly change your object to this colour combination. Simply select the object with the black arrow and then single click on the shortcut. This is very useful for garment flat drawings with multiple layers and design details (see chapter 5 and onwards).

As I explained before, the **fill and stroke squares** are a colour representation of the object you select. If you select more than one object, with different fill and stroke colours, Illustrator will not know which colour to display in the fill or stroke squares. It will replace the colour with a question mark in either or both the fill and stroke squares, depending on the colour combinations of your selected objects.

To apply colour to multiple objects:

17 In the swatch palette, select a stroke colour (keeping all the square objects on the page).

18 In the swatch palette, select a fill colour.

19 Go to the stroke square in the Tool palette and click on it to bring it to the front.

Colour swatch palettes

Illustrator uses many different types of colour swatch palettes and colour effects. Later tutorials will look at various colour effects and palettes in more detail. Here is a brief look at some of them.

You can access all colour palettes by going to Menu>Window> Swatch Libraries (Illustrator 10 and CS) or directly from the swatch palette pop-up option menu (CS only) (see picture right). Select any Pantone or other branded swatch libraries you require. Illustrator is used mainly by graphic designers and illustrators working on paper or on screen, so the choice of swatch libraries reflects this, but sadly, no fashion Pantone colour library is included. You can easily use any other library as long as your manufacturing company uses the same reference when it produces your colour lab dips.

CMYK and RGB colour modes

By default, when you open a new file, Illustrator will use the CMYK colour mode. CMYK stands for **C**yan, **M**agenta, **Y**ellow, blac**K**, which is a printing process standard, found in most digital and press printing for books and magazines. So if you are going to output your work on paper, tick the CMYK option. On the other hand, if you want to display your work on screen (website, digital portfolio and so on) you should opt for RGB (**R**ed **G**reen **B**lue). You can easily switch from one mode to the other by going to Menu>File>Document Color Mode.

To **create a new colour swatch**, click on the new swatch icon in the swatch palette.

To **modify a colour swatch:**

20 Double click on any colour swatch in the swatch palette.

21 In the swatch dialog box, adjust the sliders to change your colour.

22 Press OK to confirm.

BASIC TUTORIAL 6

The Text tool

Illustrator has very advanced text-editing capabilities. Unlike a text-editing application, Illustrator can transform text into editable objects, which enables the user to radically transform and reshape any text into something unique. You can, for example, type your name with the Text tool, selecting a common typeface, and then transform it into something unique by creating a designer brand logo. We will look at how to do this and other advanced text features in chapter 18. For now, let's learn the basic text editing features.

To create text, do the following:

1 Open the 'five squares' document.

2 In the Tool palette, select the Text tool.

3 Position your cursor on the art board, below the top square, leaving enough space to type some text (around 1cm below).

4 Single click the mouse; this will change the Text tool icon into a blinking vertical line.

5 Type in the square's colour.

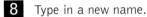

Now that you have written the colour name, you might want to change the name, the size, the typeface and the text alignment.

To rewrite text:

6 With the Text tool still selected, bring the cursor directly to the left of your text.

7 Press and drag until you have selected the whole text (or only select the part you want to change.)

8 Type in a new name.

To change the typeface and size:

9 Select the text object with the black arrow or the Text tool.

10 Go to Menu>Window>Type>Character.

11 In the Character palette select any typeface and point size that suits your style.

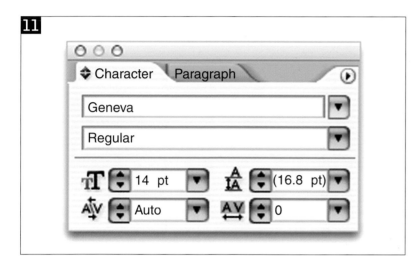

11

You can change the typeface and size directly in the Control palette (Illustrator CS2 only).

To change the typeface alignment:

12 Go to Menu>Window>Type>Paragraph.

13 In the Paragraph floating palette, click on centre alignment. This will only align the text on its path. You can notice this by the small dot having moved to the centre of the text path (under the text).

14 If your text is still not aligned with your square, do not worry about it now; leave it as it is unless it is totally off-centre, in which case move it towards the centre with the black arrow.

13

You can change the typeface alignment directly in the Control palette (Illustrator CS2 only).

Your colour name is now ready to be duplicated for the next square:

15 With the black arrow, select the first colour name.

16 Press and drag it down below the second square. Press Shift to constrain your move vertically and Alt to duplicate.

17 Release the mouse button and then the Shift and Alt keys.

18 Select the Text tool, press and drag over the text to edit it and type in the new colour name.

19 Repeat step 1 to 4 three times until you have a colour name for each square.

I hope you have noticed by now that you are creating a **colour card**! With this in mind, you might want to change the colours and names of some of the square colours and also have all the squares with a black stroke or no stroke. Remember, you can do this easily by selecting all the squares and picking the black or no-colour swatch in the swatch palette (see page 38).

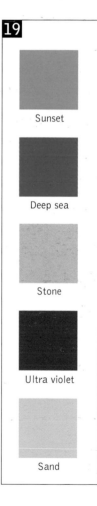

19

Sunset

Deep sea

Stone

Ultra violet

Sand

■ **Quick tip**

You can double click on a text path with the black arrow to highlight it automatically. This is faster than switching between the black arrow and the Text tool.

To align text and any other object:

Your text might still not be aligned with the squares; to change this, do the following:

 Go to Menu>Windows>Align.

21 Select all your text and colour swatch squares (Command+A or Control+A in Windows).

22 In the Align palette, tick on the Horizontal Align Centre button (if all your objects move to the centre of the page, go to the Align palette pop-up menu and un-tick Align to Artboard), then repeat the step.

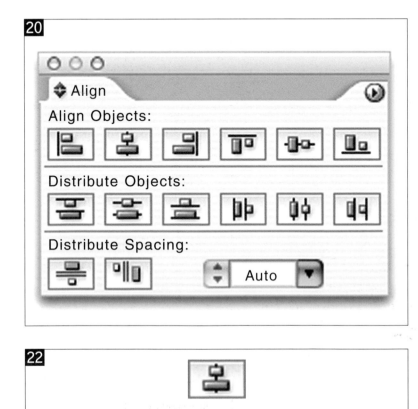

Now that your first row is aligned, you can copy it across the page to add more colour swatches to your colour card.

23 If they are not yet selected, select all the objects on the art board (Command+A).

24 With the black arrow, press and drag your selection to the right of the page, pressing Shift to constrain horizontally and Alt to duplicate.

25 Release the mouse button first and then the Shift and Alt keys.

26 Duplicate your last move three times (Command+D or Control+D Windows).

27 Change the colours, using the Swatch palette.

28 Rename the colours, using the Text tool.

29 Select All (Command+A or Control+A Windows).

30 Go to Menu>Object>Group (Command+G or Control+G Windows) to group your selection.

31 In the Align palette, tick Align to Artboard in the palette pop-up option menu, and then select Horizontal Align Centre and then Vertical Align Centre.

32 Save your document as: colour card 1 (Menu>File>Save As or Command+Shift+S or Control+ Shift+S for Windows).

You have now completed the basic tutorials and created a simple colour card. I suggest that you design a new colour card from scratch, without the help of the book, to see how much you have assimilated so far. Because the basic skills you have learned will be used all the time, it is crucial that they come naturally, without the help of a book or notes.

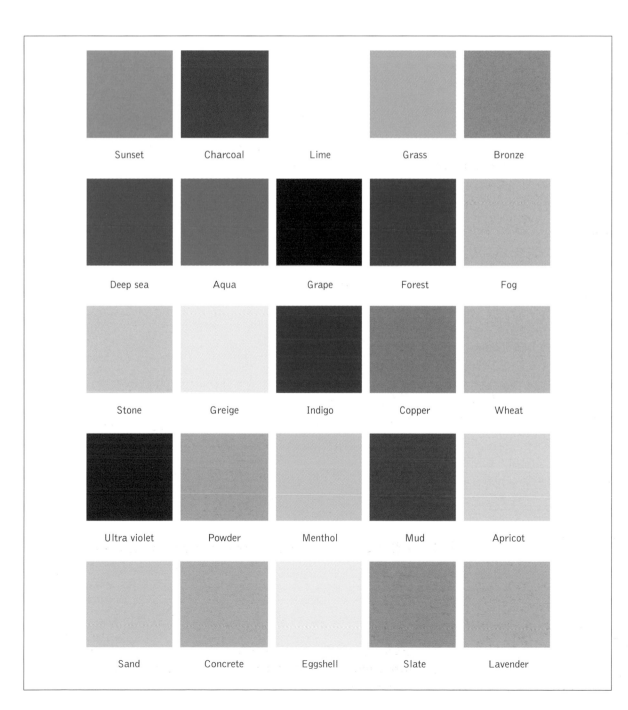

Sunset	Charcoal	Lime	Grass	Bronze
Deep sea	Aqua	Grape	Forest	Fog
Stone	Greige	Indigo	Copper	Wheat
Ultra violet	Powder	Menthol	Mud	Apricot
Sand	Concrete	Eggshell	Slate	Lavender

Simple colour card

Chapter 4
Pen Tool Tutorial

Illustrator's pen is one of the most important tools for a fashion designer creating garment flat drawings or sketches, as it is both precise and flexible. Unfortunately, the Pen tool is tricky to use, especially when drawing curves, but once mastered, it will enable designers to create great sketches.

Any shape made with a Pen tool contains segments and anchor points, just like any other object. Drawing a shape with the Pen tool is like unreeling a spool of thread: every time you single click, the thread is being anchored and wherever you move with the cursor, the thread follows you. The most basic use for the Pen tool is to single click, move, single click, move and so on. This will create a shape with straight lines.

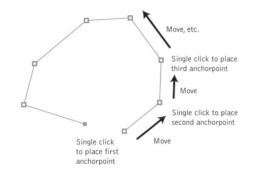

When you draw an object with the Pen tool, you can either leave it open or close it. An open shape can be useful in some cases, such as topstitch lines and other details, but open shapes can also cause problems when filled with colour. This is especially so with white fill on white canvas, since Illustrator by default always fills new objects with white and you will not be able to see the white fill against the white canvas. This can result in the fill masking any objects below.

The trickiest part when mastering the Pen tool is to draw a curve. Illustrator works with Bezier curves and it is useful to know that a Bezier curve is made of a single anchor point from which a curve handle stems out. A curve can be modified by pressing and dragging the handle's end. Curves will be shallow if the handle is close to the anchor point. On the other hand, they will be deep if the handle is long and far from the anchor point. The direction or angle of the handle influences the shape of the curve as well. It will take new users quite a while to produce smooth curves.

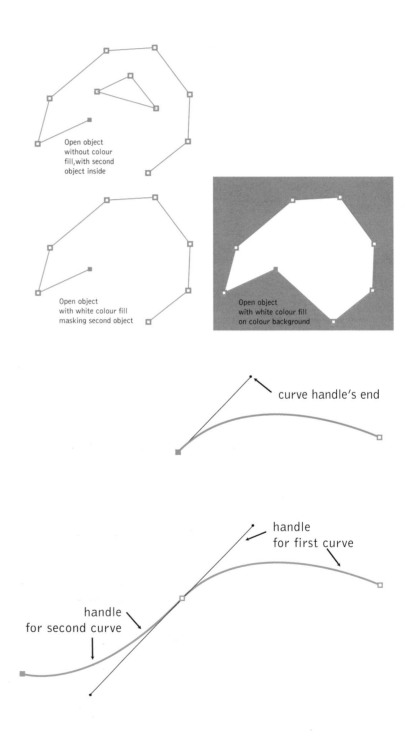

PEN TOOL TUTORIAL 1

Drawing a line, closing a shape

Since Pen tool curves are tricky, let's start by drawing a simple shape, made of straight lines:

1 Select the Pen tool.

2 On your art board, single click (make sure you do not press and drag!); this will create your first anchor point.

3 Move wherever you wish on your art board to position your second anchor point.

4 Single click again; this will draw a segment line, starting from your first anchor point and finishing at your second.

5 Move again for the next anchor point, making sure that you do not cross over the first segment.

6 Single click to create your second segment.

7 Carry on and draw a few more segments, and then start coming back towards your first anchor point.

8 To close the shape, move your mouse towards the first anchor point.

9 When you are right on top of the first anchor point, you should see the Pen tool cursor with a little hollow dot to its lower right side.

10 Only when you see the closing shape Pen tool icon can you single click the mouse to draw your final segment and close the shape.

Constrain when drawing with the Pen tool

The Pen tool can be constrained to various angles (including 45 and 90 degrees) when you move from one anchor point to the other. This constraining action will make you draw a straight line, a 45-degree line or a vertical line, depending on where you place your second anchor point. Let's create a shape containing different constrained segments.

11 With the Pen tool selected, single click your first anchor point.

12 Move left horizontally towards your second anchor point position.

13 Press Shift and then single click.

14 Release the Shift key.

15 You should now have a horizontally straight line. If not, press Command+Z (Control+Z Windows)and start again until you get a horizontally straight line.

16 Move straight up towards your third anchor point, on the same vertical line.

17 Press Shift again, single click your mouse and then release the Shift key. You should have a straight vertical line.

18 Move further up to the right at a 45-degree angle; press Shift and single click the mouse for your third anchor point. Release the Shift key.

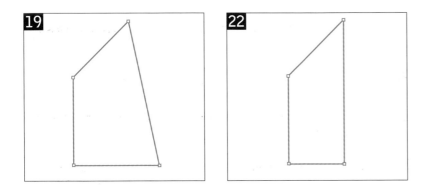

Creating open objects with the Pen tool

This is very useful for designing fashion details, such as darts, pleats or topstitches and also half garment shapes, which can be mirrored. Let's create a simple pleat to learn how to make an open object:

23 With the Pen tool selected, single click your first anchor point.

24 Move towards your second anchor point and single click to create your first segment.

25 Move again, single click to create your second segment.

26 To finish your open object, simply go toward the black arrow in the toolbox and select it.

Alternatively:

Click away while pressing Command (Control for Windows). Make sure your open object has no fill colour.

19 Come back down towards your first anchor point; wait to see the close shape icon on the Pen tool, and single click to close the shape.

20 The last segment cannot be constrained because it is next to impossible to match the constrain angles with the segment distances.

21 Select the white arrow and single click your first anchor point.

22 Press your keyboard arrow key to nudge the anchor point to the left or right to align it with the anchor point above it. You might need to change the cursor key increment to a smaller value in Menu>Illustrator>Preferences>General.

Open object

Adding anchor points to an object

An object created with the Pen tool (or any other object) can have anchor points added and deleted. This can be useful if you want to modify simple shapes or simplify complex ones. Let's start by adding anchor points to a simple object:

 Select the Rectangle tool in the Tool palette.

 Press and drag to create a rectangle.

29 Go to the Pen tool floating palette (tear it off from the Tool palette if it is not visible) and select the Add Anchor Point tool.

30 Single click any of the rectangle's segments where you want to add an anchor point.

31 Add a further three anchor points (one per segment).

32 Select the white arrow and single click one of the newly created anchor points.

33 Nudge the anchor point in a new position, either using the arrow keys or pressing and draging.

34 Move any other anchor points into new positions to create a new shape.

To delete anchor points, do the following:

35 Select the Delete Anchor Point tool.

36 Single click on any of your object's anchor points to delete it.

37 You can create a totally different shape by deleting a couple of anchor points.

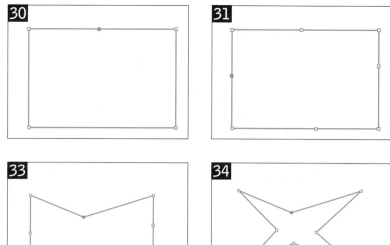

PEN TOOL TUTORIAL 2

Creating and modifying curves

This is it, the moment you all been waiting for: creating a curve with the Pen tool! Hopefully it will not be as hard as I have suggested previously. Learning how to draw straight lines has already warmed you up; you can now learn how to draw a simple curve.

1 Select the Pen tool and single click the first anchor point on your art board.

2 Move towards the second anchor point position and then press and drag the mouse. DO NOT release the mouse button.

3 You should see a set of curve handles appear, one of them next to your mouse cursor and the other away from it.

4 As long as your mouse button is pressed down, you are in control of the curve and can still shape it. Use a circular motion to adjust your curve. When you are happy with your curve shape, release the mouse button.

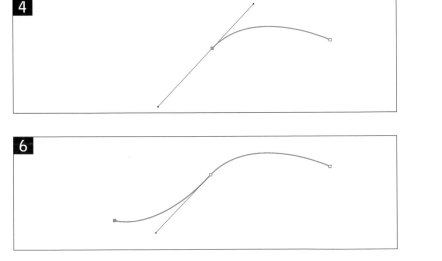

5 Move towards your next anchor point and this time simply single click the mouse. A second curve automatically appears.

6 Press Alt and click away to deselect the curved segment just created (or select the black arrow and click away).

Illustrator automatically adds a second curved segment after the first one, because when a curve is created it always contains two curve handles. The curve handle on the right manages the first curve and the one on the left the second curve.

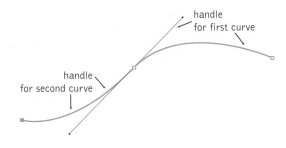

handle
for first curve

handle
for second curve

To draw a smooth second curve, make sure that it goes towards the same direction as the curve handle. We will look into this in the first fashion sketch tutorial when creating a waistline curve.

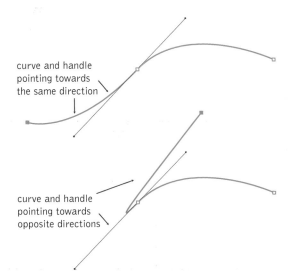

curve and handle
pointing towards
the same direction

curve and handle
pointing towards
opposite directions

To create a curve followed by a straight line, do the following:

7   Select the Pen tool and single click on the art board to place your first anchor point.

8   Move towards your second anchor point and press and drag to create a curve.

9   Release the mouse button when your curve has the correct shape.

10   Rather than moving to the next anchor point position, go over the one you just created and single click on it. (The Pen tool should have a slash sign next to it.) This will make the second curve handle disappear.

11   Move to the next anchor point position and single click the mouse. This will create a straight segment.

12   Press Command (or Control for Windows) and click away to deselect the shape (or select the black arrow and click away).

You can easily modify a curve after creating it and you can also get rid of a curve or create a curve on any anchor point.

To modify a curve, do as follows:

13   Select the white arrow and go back to the first shape you created (two curves).

14   Single click or area-select the middle anchor point (the one with the curve handles); you should now see two curve handles.

15   Chose which curve and therefore which handle you want to modify.

16   Point your mouse cursor on the chosen curve handle's end.

17   Press and drag the handle, moving in a circular motion to change the curve direction or up and down to make the curve shallower or deeper.

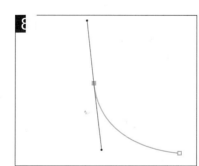

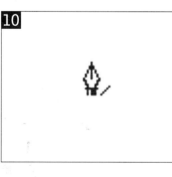

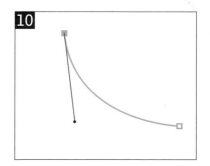

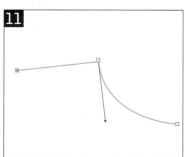

To delete an unwanted curve or to create a new one, do the following:

 18 Draw a segment with at least one curve.

19 In the pen floating palette, select the Convert Anchor Point tool.

20 Single click on the anchor point with a curve; this will convert the curve into a straight segment.

21 To create a curve on any non-curved anchor point, simply press and drag the anchor point, using the same Convert Anchor Point tool.

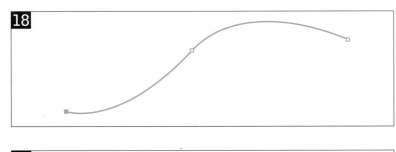

18

19

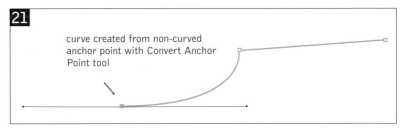

20

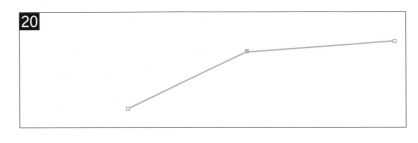

21

curve created from non-curved anchor point with Convert Anchor Point tool

That's it! Not too hard was it? I suggest that you now practise by trying to draw a fashion-based simple shape such as, for example, a collar. This will help you get the hang of drawing straight and curved lines with the Pen tool before you begin the first real fashion tutorial.

collar shape

Chapter 5
First Fashion Sketch Tutorial

Now that you have learned the basics of Illustrator, you can finally start working on garment flat drawings (also known as garment sketches). To keep things simple to begin with, you will draw a vest. See this as a block, from which you will be able to create many different designs. As you already know, the best way to draw garment sketches in Illustrator is with the Pen tool; you should now have a basic knowledge of this tool and be able to draw a simple shape.

Being able to draw garment flats in Illustrator is one thing; the main issue is that you will hopefully enjoy drawing them while using your creativity.

A few basic principles govern the way garment sketches are drawn in Illustrator:

- Always keep your anchor point count as low as possible; for example, half a vest should have no more than seven anchor points. If you have too many anchor points, segments could become uneven, curves bumpy and shapes harder to modify.
- Drawing a sketch in Illustrator is very similar to cutting a pattern on paper and anchor points are usually located at key construction lines, such as waistline, chest, hips and so on.
- A shape can be mirrored in an instant, so you only need to draw half a shape.
- Garment sketches have a minimum of two layers: a Shape layer, containing your garment outline shape, and the Details, containing all the details.

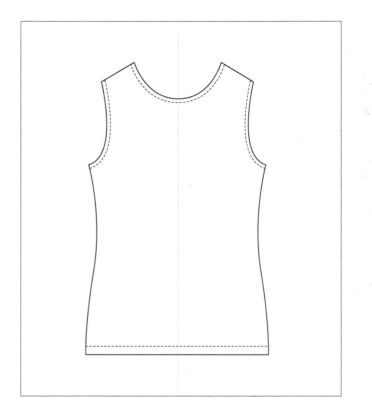

Setting up

Before you start designing the first garment sketch, you need to set up the work environment by creating a centre front line (CF), just as you would for pattern cutting. You also need to name the first layer.

To create a centre front line:

1 Create a new document named 'my first sketch'.

2 Go to Menu>Views>Show Rulers (or Command+R). You will see a set of rulers on the left and top of your art board window.

3 Bring your mouse cursor above the left ruler and then press and drag your mouse back towards the centre of your page (you should see a vertical dotted line following your mouse).

4 Release the mouse button.

5 You should now see a blue line crossing your page vertically (note that these guides do not print).

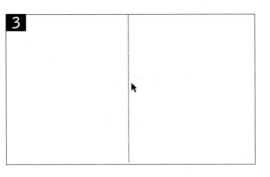

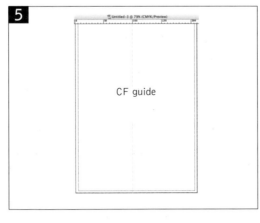

CF guide

To rename the layer:

6 If the layer palette is not visible, go to Menu>Windows>Layers.

7 In the layer palette, double click the Layer 1 text.

8 In the Layer option dialog box, highlight the text Layer 1 and rename it 'Shape'.

9 Press OK to confirm.

The vest shape

After having set up your page, you can start drawing the shape lines. Keep in mind that you will not be able to do a perfect shape right away. Just make sure that you have drawn all your anchor points, lines and curves. You will be able to retouch your shape at a later stage. Half a vest shape is constructed with seven anchor points: neck CF, side neck, shoulder, armhole, waist, hip/hem side and hip/hem CF.

10 Select the Pen tool.

11 On the centre front line (roughly a third of the way down from top of your A4 sheet), single click your first anchor point.

12 Move your Pen tool towards the left and slightly up. Single click to create the neck side anchor point. It's better to make your half neck straight for now; you will discover why later, when you mirror the shape.

13 Move the pen again towards the left, this time slightly below the last point. Single click to create your shoulder point.

14 Go below the last anchor point, slightly to the left. Press and drag to create your armhole curve. Release the mouse button. You will see two Bezier handles, but because our next segment is straight, we only need one Bezier handle, so single click the anchor point. You should now only have one Bezier handle on view.

15 Go straight below the armhole anchor point and press and drag to create the waistline curve (try to keep the Bezier handle as close to the side of the vest shape as possible). Now release the mouse button.

16 Go to the next anchor point position, moving your mouse cursor straight down, slightly to the left. Single click to place the hem side anchor point.

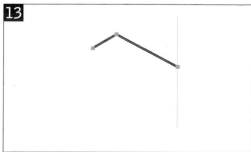

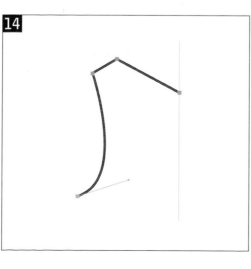

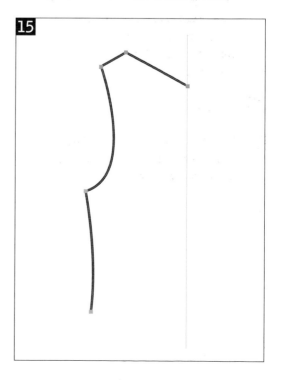

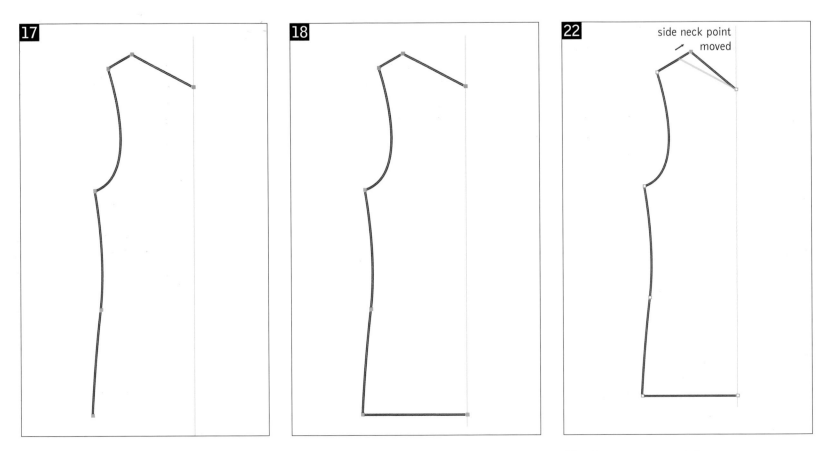

17 Finally, move your mouse back horizontally to the centre front guide line. Hold the Shift key to constrain, then single click. You have now completed your half vest shape.

18 Select the black arrow or click away+Alt to finish working with the Pen tool and this shape.

Modifying the shape

Your half shape is finished, but the top needs to be retouched. There are several ways to do this: move single or groups of anchor points, modify Bezier curves or modify straight or curved segments directly. You have already learned some of these skills in the basic tutorials for simple objects. The various techniques are explained again here in relation to garment shapes. Try to retouch and fine-tune your shape, using these techniques as appropriate:

Moving anchor points

This technique is good to use when any anchor point is out of position in relation to the shape. Quite often, when you draft the first shape you are not aware of proportions and might position a neckline point too low or a waistline too high.

To move single anchor points, do as follows:

19 Select the white arrow and position it outside your shape and close to the anchor point you want to retouch.

20 Press and drag to area-select the anchor point you want to move. (You can also single click the anchor point directly.)

21 Use the keyboard arrow keys to nudge your point in any direction or press and drag the selected anchor point freely around.

22 Release the mouse button to drop the point in its new position.

To move multiple anchor points, do as follows:

23 Select the white arrow and position it outside your shape and close to the anchor point group you want to modify.

24 Press and drag to area-select over the anchor points you want to move. (You can also single click while pressing Shift to multiple select the anchor points directly.)

25 Use the keyboard arrow keys to nudge your points in any direction or press and drag the selected anchor points freely around.

26 Release the mouse button to drop the points to their new positions.

Modify Bezier curves

Your vest shape contains two Bezier curves: the armhole and the waistline. To modify them, do as follows:

26 multiple anchor points moved

30 armhole and waist curves modified

27 Single click or area-select the armhole anchor point, using the white arrow.

28 Press and drag the curve handle's end to modify your curve.

29 Release the mouse button when you are satisfied with the curve shape.

30 To modify your waistline curve, use the same technique, pressing and dragging any of the two curve handles.

Modify a straight or curved segment directly

You can also directly modify your shape's segments, rather than the anchor points. You can, for example, move the whole hem or reshape the armhole curve directly, without touching the Bezier handles. Let's start by modifying a straight segment:

31 Select the white arrow.

32 Press and drag any straight segment you wish (neck, shoulder or hem).

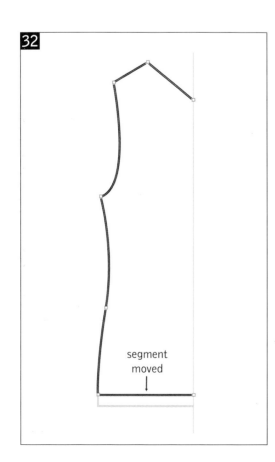

32

segment
moved
↓

33 Release the mouse button.

Use the same technique to modify a curved segment, but remember that you will not be able to move the curve anywhere; you can only change its shape between the two anchor points, which will themselves remain static.

Averaging anchor points

Averaging is the technique used to align two or more anchor points on a vertical or horizontal axis, or both. This technique will be used extensively at different stages when designing garment flats. Before mirroring your half vest shape, you will need to average vertically the first and last anchor points. When you mirror the half vest shape, it must be flush with the centre front line so that the mirrored shape will connect with the original perfectly.

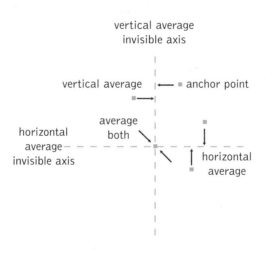

vertical average
invisible axis

vertical average ←■ anchor point
■→

average
both

horizontal
average —
invisible axis

horizontal
average

To average anchor points, do as follows:

34 Select the white arrow and either area-select both the first and last anchor points or single click each of them while pressing Shift.

35 Go to Menu>Object>Path> Average (Command+Alt+J or Control+Alt+J for Windows).

36 In the dialog box, select Vertical.

37 Press OK to confirm.

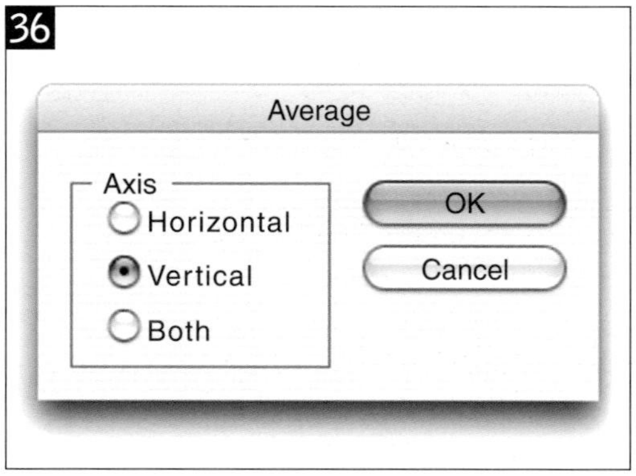

36

Average

Axis
○ Horizontal
● Vertical
○ Both

OK
Cancel

38 Make sure that your two anchor points are flush with the CF line; if not, nudge them with the keyboard arrows.

■ Quick tip

When averaging, you can also use the context menu. Simply select the anchor points to be averaged, right click the mouse and select Average in the context menu.

Aligning your shape with the CF guide line

Illustrator has a snap to grid feature, which will help you snap your shape to the CF guide line. To use the snap to grid feature, do as follows:

39 Go to Menu>View>Guides>Clear Guide.

40 Go to Menu>Illustrator>Preferences> General (or Command+K).

41 Select Guides & Grid. For Gridline every, type in 10 and for Subdivisions type 1. Press OK to confirm.

42 Go to Menu>View>Show Grid (or Command+').

43 Drag and drop a vertical guide in the middle of your page, making sure it snaps with the grid.

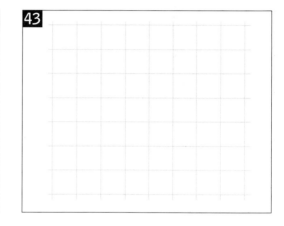

44 Select your shape with the black arrow and move it towards the guide line until it snaps to it.

Mirroring a shape

Now that your half shape is aligned with the CF line, you can mirror it:

45 Select your shape either with the black arrow or Command+A (Control+A for Windows).

46 Select the Reflect tool, which is found embedded with the Rotate tool. (If you are working with an Illustrator version below 10, the Reflect tool will be located in a different place within the tool box.)

47 When you have picked up the Reflect tool, a target icon appears in the centre of your selected shape. This target is the centre of your reflection. Because in this case the CF line is the centre of rotation, you will need to move the target by simply single clicking on the CF line, anywhere between your shape's first and last anchor points.

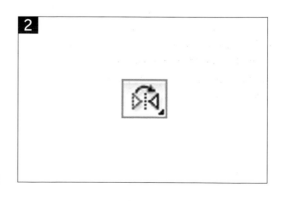

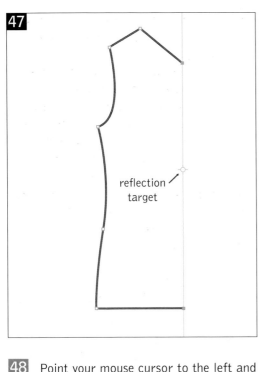

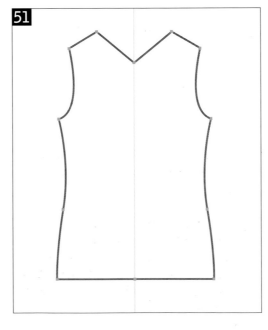

48   Point your mouse cursor to the left and slightly above your shape.

49   Press and drag your mouse in a clockwise circular motion; your mirrored shape is moving away from its original. As long as you keep your mouse button pressed, you are in control.

50   Move your shape towards its resting position and press Shift to constrain the move to horizontal and Alt to duplicate your original shape.

51   Release the mouse button and then the Shift and Alt keys.

If your shape is not mirrored properly, you might not have pressed the Shift key correctly. If you only have the reflected shape, having lost the original one, then you did not press the Alt key properly. Just press Command+Z and start again.

Now that your shape is mirrored, you need to join it. Right now, both open shapes are separated from each other.

To join two open shapes, do the following:

52   Select the white arrow.

53   From above and outside the shapes, press and drag to area-select the two centre neck end anchor points.

54   If the two points seem to be distant from each other you will need to average them by going to Menu>Object> Path>Average (Command+Alt+J or Control+Alt+J for Windows).

55   Tick Both in the dialog box.

56   Go to Menu>Objects>Path>Join (Command+J or Control+J for Windows). Tick Corner in the dialog box

57   Repeat step 1 to 4 for the two end anchor points, located at the centre front hem.

58   Your shape is now a single object. To verify this, select it with the black arrow; a bounding box should now frame the entire shape.

56

Join

Points
◉ Corner
○ Smooth

OK
Cancel

■ Quick tip

Quite often, when you try to join two anchor points, you might get the following error message:

To join, you must select two open endpoints. If they are not on the same path, they cannot be on text paths nor inside graphs, and if both of them are grouped, they must be in the same group.

☐ Don't Show Again   OK

In most cases, it's due to the fact that you have selected more than two end anchor points. This can also be due to 'stray points'.

Stray anchor points are anchor points without a segment. These are often the result of deleting a segment, but not the anchor points, with the white arrow. These stray points are invisible and can only be viewed by either selecting them or in preview mode (Menu>View> Outline or Command+Y, Control+Y for Windows). You can automatically select and delete all stray points by going to: Menu>Select>Object>Stray Points, then pressing backspace to delete them.

62

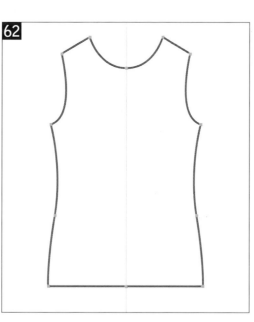

To change the V neck into a round neck, do as follows:

59 Select the Convert Anchor Point tool.

60 Press and drag the CF neck anchor point to create a Bezier curve.

61 You might get a strange-looking curve; the trick is to perform a circular motion clockwise or anticlockwise with the mouse while still pressing the mouse button.

62 With the mouse button still down, press the Shift key to constrain the curve on a horizontal line. This will make the two sides of your neck stay even. When your curve is nice and even, release the mouse button.

Now that your vest is finished and a single object, you can modify it with the bounding box, just as you have learned in the basic tutorial. Quite often, half shapes can look deceptively good, but once they are mirrored they can be too wide or too skinny. A good way to work this out is to mirror your half shape and check it. If there is a problem, delete the mirrored side and alter the original shape to mirror it again.

It is important that your shape is finalized before you start working on the design details, so make any necessary modifications before going any further.

■ Quick tip

It is better to draw a neck with a single curve in the middle rather than one on each side. This is why you have designed the half vest shape with a straight segment and transformed it into a curve once both sides of the neck were joined. The main advantage is that a single curved neckline can be made deeper or shallower without losing its shape.

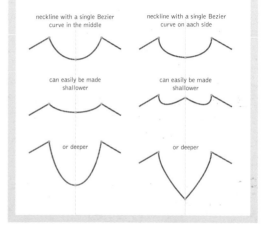

The detail layer

A fashion sketch requires at least two layers: one for the shape and a second for the details. This allows you to lock the shape layer while you work on the details. Illustrator allows you to create as many layers as you want, but I recommend that you keep your layers clearly labeled to avoid wasting time trying to find which layer contains what element. A layer can also be made invisible while another remains visible, enabling you, for example, to view a layer's content more clearly. Remember that to work in one layer or another, you first need to select it by single clicking its name in the layer palette.

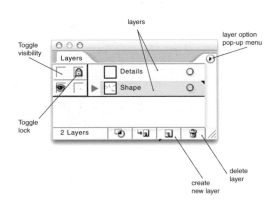

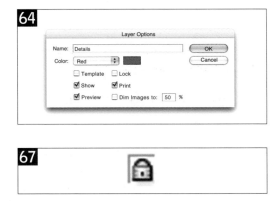

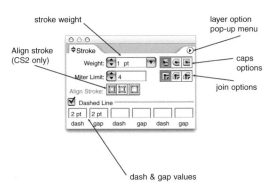

To create a new layer, do as follows:

63 In the layer floating palette, either single click the New Layer icon or, in the layer option pop-up menu, select a new layer.

64 If you have clicked the New Layer icon, you should see a new layer in the palette. Double click it. In the layer option dialog box, type Details in the Name box. Press OK to confirm.

65 If you selected New Layer in the layer option menu, a new layer option dialog box appears. In the Layer option, type Details in the Name box.

66 Press OK to confirm.

67 In the Layer palette's Shape layer, tick the Toggle lock box; you should see a padlock appearing. You Shape layer is now locked.

Topstitching

Since this is your first garment sketch, you will only design a simple topstitch line, using the stroke palette, which can handle a fair amount of topstitch size and style. Let's start by drawing the hem topstitch line:

68 On the Details layer, select the Pen tool.

69 Point the mouse cursor towards the vest hem on the left-hand side, slightly above the hem.

70 Single click your first anchor point and move to the hem's right-hand side, trying to keep the same distance above the hem.

71 Press and hold the Shift key, then single click the second anchor point. Press Command +click away or select the black arrow.

72 With the black arrow, select the segment you just created.

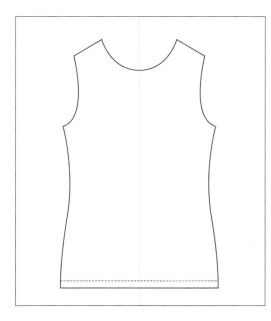

Neck and armhole details

This tutorial does not deal with neck ribbing yet, the subject being covered in the more advanced T-shirt tutorial (pages 108–115). The neck ribbing will be replaced with a simple topstitch line. The armhole will also have a single topstitch. Rather than draw the armhole and neck topstitch from scratch, you will copy and paste the shape curves, altering them if necessary. This is the simplest but crudest way to draw a curved parallel line. As you progress in the garment tutorials, you will learn a more sophisticated technique.

To use the shape lines to create a topstitch, do as follows:

77 In the layer palette, select the Shape layer by single clicking it (you should see a colour highlight over it to confirm this).

78 Single click padlock to unlock the layer.

79 Before you proceed further, go into the layer palette option menu and make sure that Paste Remembers Layers is un-ticked. If it isn't, go over it and single click it to un-tick it.

80 Single click the neck CF anchor point with the white arrow to select it.

81 Press Command+C (or Control+C for Windows) or go to Menu>Edit>Copy.

82 In the Layer palette, on the Shape layer, single click the Toggles lock box.

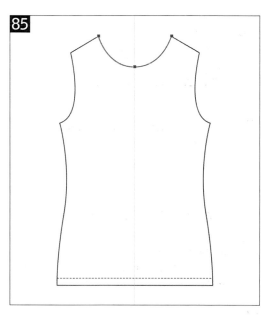

73 Give the segment a black stroke and no fill colour.

74 In the Stroke palette, tick Dashed Line. (If you do not see it, go to the palette option menu and select Show option.)

75 Input a value for dash and gap. Illustrator by default uses 12pt as a dash, which is far too big for a garment topstitch. A good average topstitch combination is 2pt for the dash and gap.

76 Change the cap style to Round Cap, to to give a more realistic topstitch look.

83 Single click the Detail layer to make it active.

84 Press Command+F (Control+F windows) or go to Menu>Edit>Paste in front.

85 Your copied neckline has pasted itself in its original position on top of the shape in the Detail layer.

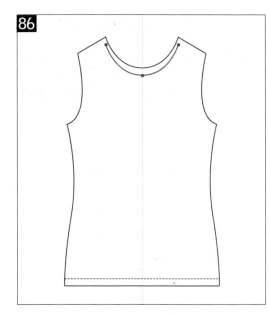

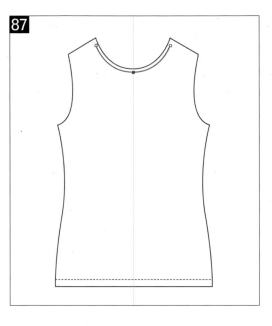

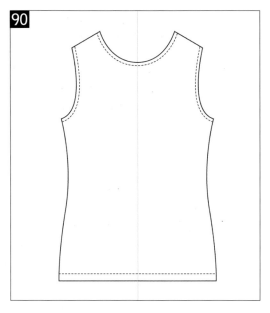

86 Nudge the new neckline down to where you want to have the topstitching, using the down arrow key.

87 With the white arrow, select the new neckline's centre anchor point and nudge it up with the arrow key until it is parallel to the original neckline.

88 Reposition both side anchor points, as shown.

89 Select the new neckline with the black arrow. In the Stroke palette, tick Dashed Line, select Round Cap and type in 2pt for dash and gap.

90 Repeat steps from 1 to 13 for the two armhole topstitch lines.

■ **Quick tip**

To work faster, use the Eyedropper tool to clone a topstitch style onto any other plain stroke line. To do so, select with the black arrow the line you want to apply cloning to and then select the Eyedropper tool; single click the topstitch (for example the hem line). This will clone the hem line topstitch style (cap, dash and stroke values) onto your selected line.

Your first sketch is now finished. It is a very simple design, containing only one detail feature, since this tutorial is mainly about learning the very basics of garment sketch in Illustrator.

Chapter 6
Skirt Sketch Tutorial

From this stage on, the garment sketch tutorials do not include detailed explanations of simple and repetitive tasks you've already mastered (such as retouching a shape, mirroring a shape, creating a new layer and so on). If you have forgotten how to do these basic tasks, go back to the first fashion sketch tutorial. From now on, these tasks will only be mentioned by name. From this point on, all garment sketch tutorials, including this one, will only contain detailed explanations of new skills to be learned or issues specific to the tutorial.

The skirt shape you are going to create is a pretty straightforward design. Nevertheless, you will learn how to work with a dummy template, make a front and back view and draw a simple zipper and shaped darts.

Working with a dummy template

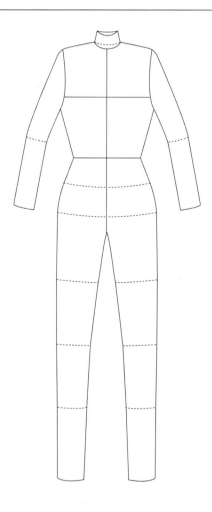

When you design garment sketches on a computer with Illustrator, it can be difficult to get a good sense of their proportions and scale. Factories often make samples based on garment flat drawings, so delivering designs with the right proportions can save a lot of time and avoid nasty surprises when receiving counter samples. Using a template dummy is a good way to keep your drawings in proportion. You can either create your own dummy or scan the one shown here. Make sure your final dummy's colour is not black, to avoid confusion with your drawings. (The dummy pictured is black to make it easier to scan!) You can easily fade it or change its colour in Photoshop or any other image-editing software. When you select or scan a dummy, keep the file size low (scan it at 150dpi in greyscale).

To place a dummy on the art board, do as follows:

 1 Create a new document (A4 portrait).

2 Go to Menu>File>Place (or open your dummy directly in Illustrator, as you would with any other file).

3 Position your dummy image in the centre of your A4 page.

4 In the layer menu, change the layer name to 'Dummy' and lock the layer.

■ Quick tip

The dummy template cannot always be fully used to draw certain garments. With this tutorial's skirt, for example, the dummy legs are too spread open to fit the shape. Only the waist, hip and knee lines will be useful.

Designing the shape

As with the previous tutorial, start by drawing the garment shape:

5 Create a new layer and name it 'Shape'.

6 Make sure the rulers are visible; if they are not, press Command+R (or Control+R windows).

7 Press and drag a vertical guide line right on top of your dummy's centre front.

8 With the Pen tool and from the centre front line, single click your first anchor point where your skirt waistband should be.

9 Draw your half shape with four more anchor points (side waist, hip, hem side and hem CF), following the dummy's coordinates. To be able to see the dummy under your shape layer, make sure your half shape has no fill colour.

10 Select the black arrow or press Command while clicking away to deselect your half shape.

11 Retouch your shape if necessary.

12 With the black arrow, select your entire shape.

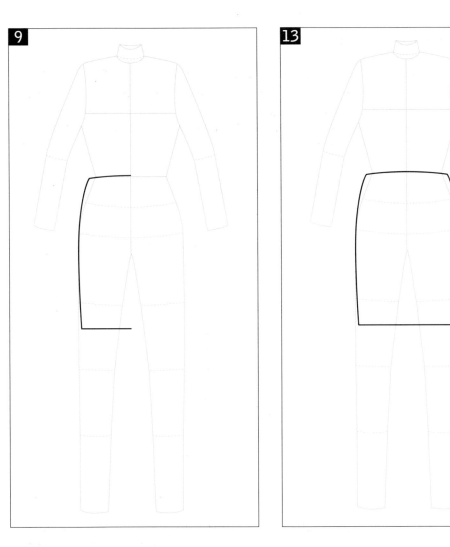

13 Select the Reflect tool and mirror your shape.

14 With the white arrow, select the two end anchor points on the waist CF and hem CF and join them, using the Average and Join Command (Command+Alt+J) and (Command+J).

Your shape is now ready. At this stage, you do not need the dummy any more and can hide it by ticking the Toggle Visibility icon in the Dummy layer.

Designing the details

This skirt has very few details, but feel free to experiment and create more. This tutorial is about learning how to draw a front and a back view, using the same shape and some of the details. This technique is used throughout the garment sketch tutorials; it helps designers to work faster by not having to draw one shape for the front view and another for the back. You might have noticed that the shape pictured has a convex waistline. The convex line suits both the front and back view of the skirt.

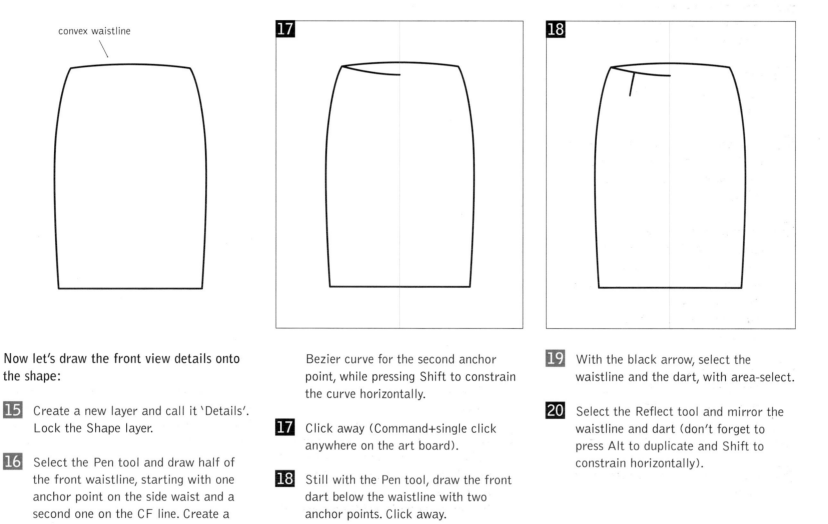

Now let's draw the front view details onto the shape:

15 Create a new layer and call it 'Details'. Lock the Shape layer.

16 Select the Pen tool and draw half of the front waistline, starting with one anchor point on the side waist and a second one on the CF line. Create a

Bezier curve for the second anchor point, while pressing Shift to constrain the curve horizontally.

17 Click away (Command+single click anywhere on the art board).

18 Still with the Pen tool, draw the front dart below the waistline with two anchor points. Click away.

19 With the black arrow, select the waistline and the dart, with area-select.

20 Select the Reflect tool and mirror the waistline and dart (don't forget to press Alt to duplicate and Shift to constrain horizontally).

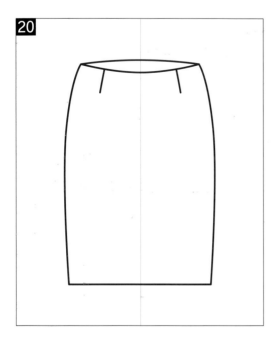

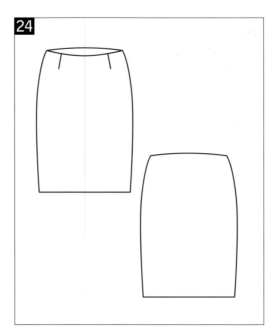

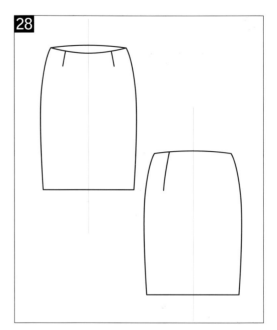

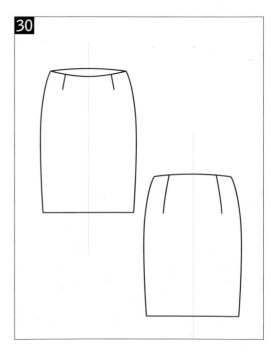

To use the front shape for the back view, do as follows:

21 In the Layer palette, lock the Detail layer and release the Shape layer.

22 Select the Shape layer by single-clicking it.

23 With the black arrow, select the shape.

24 Press and drag the shape towards the lower right. Press Shift to constrain to a 45-degree angle and Alt to duplicate the shape. Release the mouse button, then the Alt and Shift keys.

25 Press and drag a vertical guide line to the middle of the skirt back view.

26 Lock the Shape layer and release the Detail layer.

You can now draw the details on the back shape:

27 Select the Detail layer by clicking on it.

28 Select the Pen tool and draw the back dart with two anchor points as before. Click away.

29 With the black arrow, select the back dart.

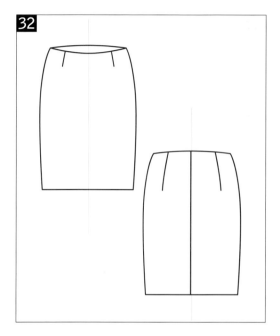

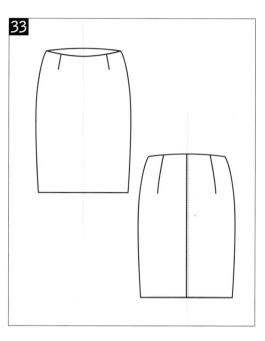

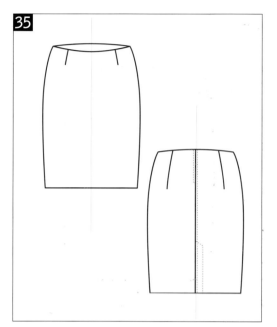

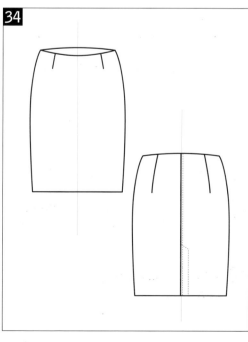

30   Select the Reflect tool and mirror the dart first, using the CB (centre back) as the reflection target. Press Alt to duplicate and Shift to constrain.

31   Select the Pen tool again and draw the CB cut line with two anchor points. (Press Shift while doing this to constrain to a vertical line.)

32   Click away to finish the line.

33   With the black arrow, select the line you have just drawn. Press and drag it to the right; press Alt to duplicate and Shift to constrain. Set the stroke to dash; type in 2pt for dash and gap, and select Round Caps and a stroke weight of 0.5pt.

34   With the Pen tool, draw the back vent with three anchor points. Click away to finish the vent.

35   Still with the Pen tool, draw the zip topstitch with three anchor points. Click away to deselect it. Both the vent and the zip topstitch should automatically be topstitched; if not, use the Eyedropper tool to clone the topstitch from the CB stitch line.

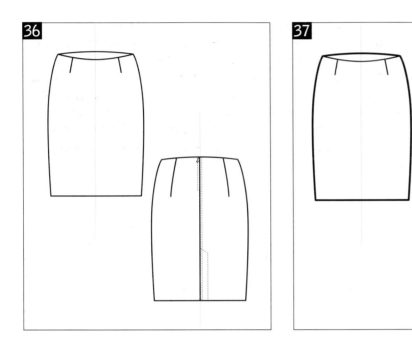

36 Draw a simple zip puller with three anchor points. This is the easiest way to depict an invisible zip. Click away to finish the zip puller. The puller might be topstitched like the previous object you drew). Un-tick the dash box in the Stroke palette when your zip puller is selected and also make the stroke thicker (1pt).

37 Finally, release the Shape layer; select both shapes and give them a stroke of 2pt to make them stand out.

You now have finished the skirt design. If you have struggled, it is probably because the step-by-step instructions are less detailed than in the vest tutorial. Refer to the vest tutorial if you are stuck at any stage.

Chapter 7
Trousers Sketch Tutorial

Hopefully, you managed to go through the previous tutorial without having to refer to detailed step-by-step explanations from the first sketch tutorial. The idea is for you to start focusing on design issues rather than reading through lengthy descriptions of how to use such and such a tool or how to manipulate your shape in such and such a way. If, on the other hand, you needed to refer to the first sketch tutorial, this is only normal, since there are so many things to learn initially. Remember that the process of designing garment sketches in Illustrator, whether simple or complicated, works with the same basic principle as described in detail in the first sketch tutorial.

In this trousers tutorial, you will learn several new skills and create new design details, such as four-hole buttons, welt pockets and bar-tack stitches. The best way to design a trouser shape in Illustrator is to use the same construction lines (or anchor points) as one would for pattern cutting. In other words, the techniques are the same as those we have learned with the vest and the skirt. With these anchor point placed in the right position, you will be able to create many different trousers shapes from your original design simply by moving anchor points around.

Designing the shape

The shape you will create is a simple straight-leg pair of men's trousers, which can easily be modified into a women's shape. You can use the dummy to get the proportions right.

Let's start by drawing the leg:

1 Create a new document and drag a vertical guide line to the centre of the page. Name the first layer 'Shape'.

2 (Optional) Create a new layer, name it 'Dummy' and place the dummy onto it. Make sure that the Dummy layer is below the Shape layer and locked.

3 Select the Pen tool and draw the front left leg with eight anchor points, starting with the CB waist, then side waist, hip, outer knee, outer hem, inner hem, inside knee and crotch.

4 The following anchor points should have curves: hip and crotch. The other anchor points have straight segments.

5 Adjust your shape with the white arrow, if necessary.

6 Select the whole shape (either with the black arrow or with select all).

7 Select the Reflect tool; move the reflect target to the CF line, and mirror the shape while pressing both the Alt and Shift keys.

8 Release the Alt and Shift keys and then the mouse button.

9 With the white arrow, select the two CB waist end anchor point using area-select (press and drag over them).

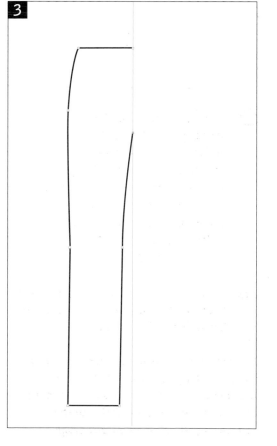

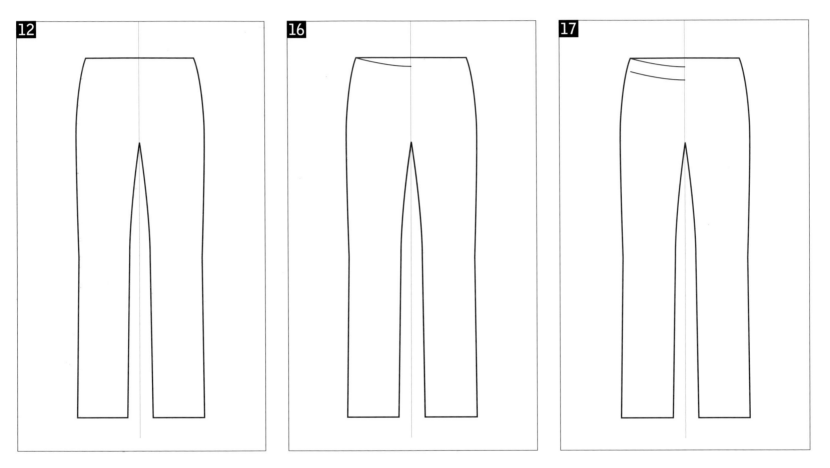

10
Average (Command+Alt+J) and then join (Command+J) the two end anchor points. Repeat this for the two other end anchor points (left and right crotch).

11
Your shape is now one object.

12
Select the shape with the black arrow, using the bounding box to change its proportions if necessary.

Designing the details

Draw the waistband and belt loops as follows:

13
Create a new layer and call it 'Details'. Lock the Shape layer and Dummy layer.

14
Select the Pen tool and draw half of the front waistline, starting with one anchor point on the side waist and a second one on the CF line. Create a

Bezier curve for the second anchor point while pressing Shift to constrain the curve horizontally.

15
Click away to finish the half front waistline.

16
Give the waistline a black stroke with 1pt weight and no fill.

17
Rather than draw the waistband from scratch, select the waistline segment

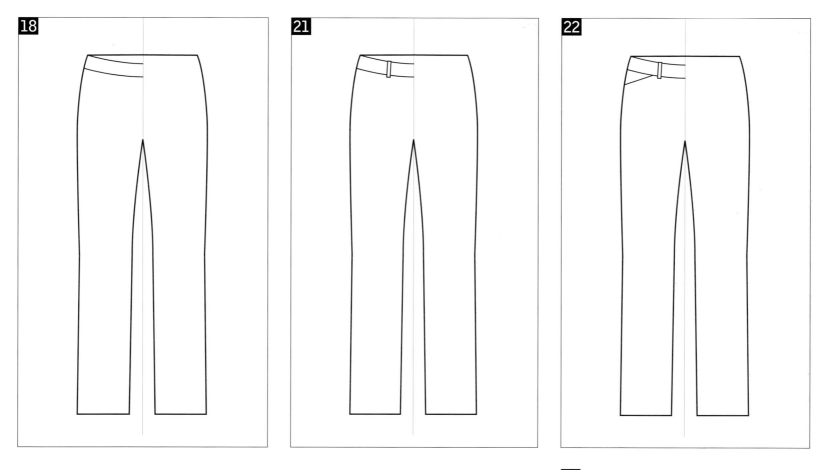

with the black arrow and drag it down while pressing the Shift and Alt keys. Release the mouse button.

18 With the white arrow, select the waistband's left anchor point and nudge it with the left arrow key or move it to the side of waist. Make sure the curve is still parallel with the waistline; if not, you can modify the waistband curve on the CF anchor point.

Draw the belt loop as follows:

19 Select the Rectangle tool; place it on the waistband, and press and drag to create a simple belt loop.

20 Use the bounding box to modify your belt loop if you did not get the size and proportions right. You can also slightly rotate the belt loop so it is perpendicular to the waistline.

21 Give the belt loop a white fill to cover the waistline and waistband, overlapping segments.

Design the front pocket, with bar-tacks, as follows:

22 Select the Pen tool and draw the front pocket, with two anchor points. Click away. Make sure this segment has no fill colour.

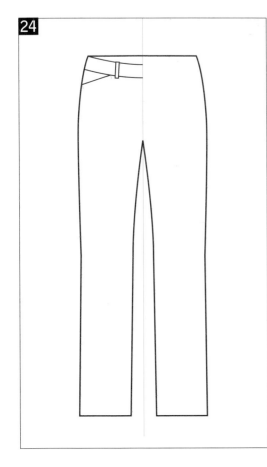

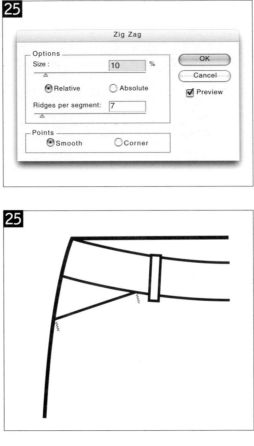

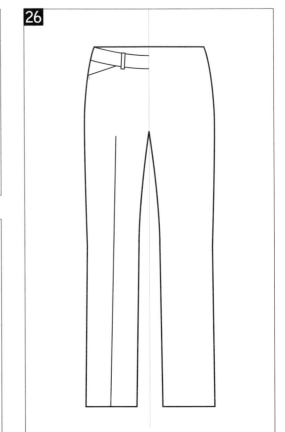

 23 Draw two small segments, using two anchor points for each, where your pocket bar-tack will be placed.

24 Select both segments with the black arrow; in the Stroke palette select a stroke weight of 0.25pt.

25 With both segments still selected, go to Menu>Filter>Distort>Zig Zag. In the dialog box; tick on Preview to see how the zigzag will look on the segments

(you might need to move the dialog box to the side to see the segments better). The zigzag in the flat drawing pictured has a size of 10 per cent, is relative, and has seven ridges per segment and smooth points. Make sure your stroke has a round cap and join.

You can also try different types of zigzag styles if you wish to have another look and feel for your trousers.

You now need to draw the crease line and mirror the front details:

26 Select the Pen tool and draw a crease line, using two anchor points. Click away. (Make sure your crease line ends up in the middle of your hemline.) Also make sure the crease line has no fill colour.

27 With the black arrow, select all front details.

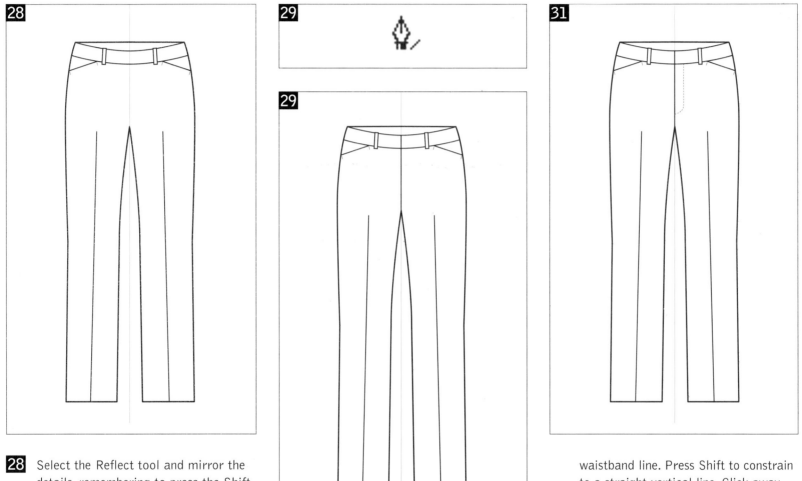

28 Select the Reflect tool and mirror the details, remembering to press the Shift and Alt keys. Release the mouse button and then the Alt and Shift keys.

Finish by drawing the front fly zipper:

29 With the Pen tool, draw the CF line by placing two anchor points, starting from the CF waistline (you can link the CF line with the CF waistline anchor point by clicking on it when the Pen tool has a forward dash next to it). Click away.

30 From the CF line, slightly above the crotch, click your first anchor point and then move upwards and to the right to create the second anchor point with a Bezier curve. The last anchor point should be placed right on top of the waistband line. Press Shift to constrain to a straight vertical line. Click away.

31 Select your newly created fly topstitch with the black arrow and tick Dashed Line in the Stroke palette; type in a Dash and Gap value of 2pt. Give your fly topstitch a stroke weight of 0.25pt and select round cap and join.

Your trousers front view is now completed. Feel free to add any details you wish.

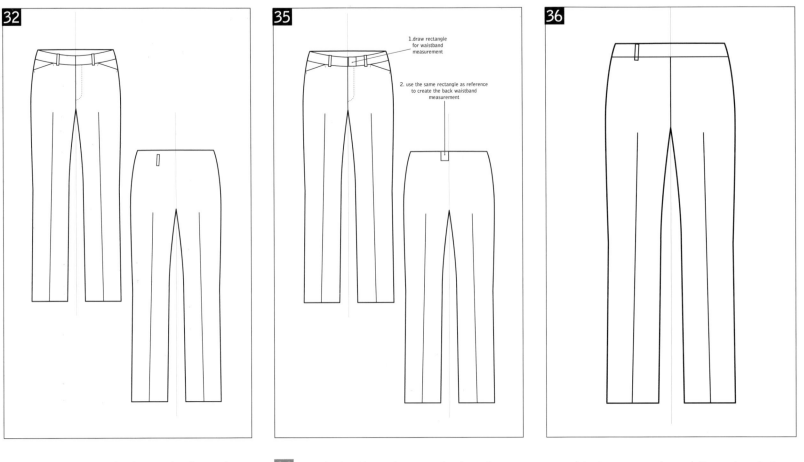

The next step is to duplicate the front shape for the back view, and salvage some details for the back view:

32 Unlock the Shape layer and, with the black arrow, select the trousers shape, the left belt loop and both crease lines.

33 Press and drag the shape towards the lower right. Press Shift to constrain to a 45-degree angle and Alt to duplicate. Release the mouse.

34 Lock the Shape layer and select the Pen tool, using it to draw the waistband pressing the Shift key when clicking the second anchor point to constrain it to a horizontal line. Click away.

35 To make sure that the back waistband is the same size as the front one, do the following: select the Rectangle tool and press and drag a rectangle over the front waistband, making sure that its height is the same as the waistband. Select the

black arrow and move the rectangle to the back waistband, aligning its top line with the top waistline. If necessary, select the back waistband line you just drew and nudge it with the up or down arrow keys. Delete the rectangle when finished.

36 Select the Pen tool and use it to draw the CB line with two anchor points, pressing the Shift key when clicking the second anchor point to constrain to a vertical line.

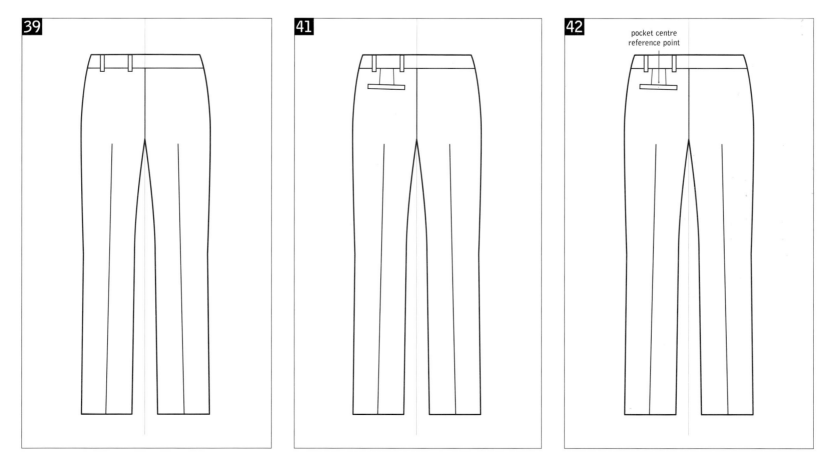

37 The belt loop you copied earlier from the front details is now below the waistband segment. To bring it back on top, go to Menu>Object>Arrange>Bring to Front (Command+Shift+] or Control+Shift+] for Windows).

38 Move the rectangle into position. You will also need to rotate it back, using the bounding box, to have it perpendicular to the back waistline.

39 Press and drag the belt loop towards the CB while pressing the Alt and Shift keys. You now should have two belt loops, one close to the left edge and one close to the CB line.

You are now going to draw the back pocket with all its details, except the button:

40 Start by drawing the pocket welt with the Rectangle tool (rotate the jet slightly clockwise).

41 Select the Pen tool and draw two back darts, with two anchor points each, going from the pocket jet to the waistband. Click away after each dart is completed.

42 With the black arrow, select the jet pocket. Press and drag a vertical guide line in the centre of jet, using the centre point on the welt as reference for your guide line.

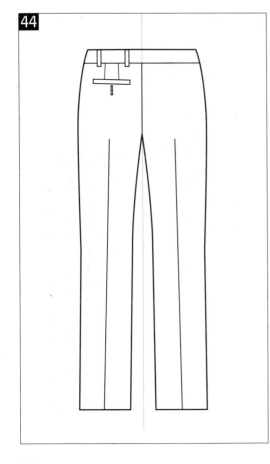

43 Now select the Rectangle tool and from this new guide line, below the jet, press and drag to create a simple buttonhole.

44 With the buttonhole selected, go to Menu>Filter>Distort>Zig Zag. In the dialog box, tick on preview. The zigzag pictured has a size of five percent, is relative, has 30 ridges per segment and the points are smooth. Make sure your stroke has a round cap and join.

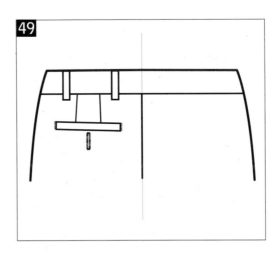

45 Select the white arrow and with it pick the side segments of both welts (using the Shift key to multiple select).

46 Copy them (Command+C or Menu>Edit>Copy).

47 Paste them in front (Command+F or Menu>Edit>Paste in front).

48 To transform both segments into bar-tacks, go to Menu>Filter>Distort>Zig Zag. In the dialog box, tick on preview. The zigzag pictured has a size of five percent, is relative, has 14 ridges per segment and the points are smooth. Make sure your stroke has a round cap and join.

49 The pocket welt hides both bar-tacks. You need to nudge them to the left and right and give them a stroke of 0.25pt.

Quick tip

When you created the buttonhole rectangle, you had to align it vertically with a guide line. To make this process easier, press the Alt key before you press and drag your rectangle; this will make the rectangle grow from the centre rather than the side.

usually when you press and drag a rectangle, it grows from the side

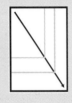

If you press Alt while you press and drag the rectangle will grow from the centre

Now let's create the four-hole button:

50 Select the Ellipse tool; move to a free space close to the back pocket buttonhole (but not on it); press and drag, while holding the Shift key to constrain into a circle.

51 Release the mouse button and then Shift when the size of the circle looks proportional to the pocket and buttonhole.

52 With the Ellipse tool still selected, go over the centre point of your first circle. Press the Alt key, to grow the circle from the centre. Press and drag a second circle, slightly smaller than the first one (don't forget to press Shift to constrain).

53 Release the mouse button and then the Alt and Shift keys.

54 Create a small circle inside the button, making its stroke weight no more than 0.10pt.

55 Select the black arrow; press and drag the small circle to the right with the Alt and Shift keys to constrain and duplicate it.

56 Select both small circles; press and drag them and duplicate them below to create two more buttonholes.

57 With the black arrow, select the four small circles and group them: Menu>Object>Group (or Command+G or Option+G for Windows).

58 Still with the black arrow, select the four buttonholes and the two outer circles; in the Align palette, under Align Objects press Vertical Align Centre and Horizontal Align Centre.

59 Finish by grouping your entire button (Command+G) and moving it to the correct position.

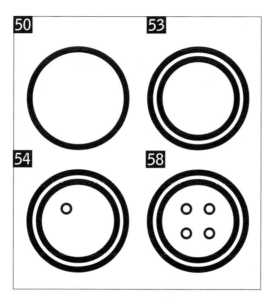

You can now mirror and duplicate the whole pocket and darts to the right side, if necessary. If you only want to have one pocket, mirror it without duplicating it (because a single pocket is usually located on the right-hand side).

You have now finished the trousers front and back view. At this stage you should retouch any flaws or design details. For example, you could do the following:

60 The back crotch is usually lower than the front. To lower it, unlock the Shape layer and area-select the crotch and the CB line, nudging them with the keyboard arrows.

61 Check all stroke weights; you could make the shape outline stroke thicker (2pts) and other lines thinner.

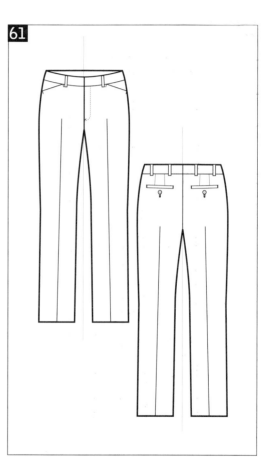

■ Quick tip

To work even faster, you can use the keyboard shortcuts to select different tools. This avoids the back and forth mouse motion from the art board to the Tool palette. Tools keyboard shortcuts are usually the first letter of a tool, for example the Pen tool shortcut is the P key. From now on and until the last garment sketch tutorial tool shortcuts will be included to help you memorize them.

Chapter 8
Shirt Sketch Tutorial

We now have designed three sketches from scratch; your confidence and skill level should start to be high! Our next shape is a classic shirt design for womenswear. You can easily transform it into a classic men's shirt, if necessary. One of the key skills you are going to learn is how to design perfect parallel-curve stitch lines, using the outline stroke technique. Other skills will include how to design folded sleeves. As before, we will start by designing the shape.

Designing the shape

Shirts usually are designed with folded arms, since they tend to have a shallow sleeve curve, resulting in the sleeve coming out from the head at an angle nearly parallel to the shoulder seam. If the sleeve is not folded, this will result in a shirt shape that takes a lot of space widthwise. You will design the front half shape in a way that enables you to use it for the back view without any modification:

1 Create a new document and drag a vertical guide line in the centre of the A4 page for your CF line. Name the first layer 'Shape'.

2 (Optional) Create a new layer, name it 'Dummy' and place the dummy into it. Make sure that the Dummy layer is below the Shape layer and that it is locked.

3 With the Pen tool (P) draw half the shape, using 13 anchor points, starting with the CB collar then side collar, side neck, shoulder edge, top sleeve, sleeve fold, outer cuff, inner cuff, inner fold, underarm, waist, hip and CF hem. Click away.

4 The following anchor points should have curves: hip and CF hem. All other anchor points have straight segments.

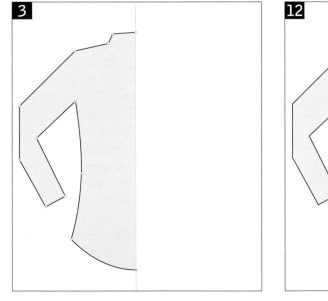

5 Adjust your shape with the white arrow (A), if necessary.

6 Select the shape, either with the black arrow (V) or with Select All

7 Select the Reflect tool (O); move the reflect target to the CF line and mirror the shape while pressing the Alt and Shift keys.

8   Release the Alt and Shift keys and then the mouse button.

9   Select the white arrow (A). Select the two CB collar end anchor points, using an area-select (press and drag over them).

10 Average (Command+Alt+J) and then join (Command +J) the two end anchor points. Repeat this for the two other end anchor points (left and right CF hem).

11 Your shape should now be a single object.

12 With the black arrow (V), you can select the shape and, with the bounding box, change its proportions if necessary.

■ **Quick tip**

When you create a new document in Illustrator and draw a shape, by default it will be filled with white and have a black stroke. Because Illustrator uses a white background, you cannot differentiate the background from a white fill or a transparent fill (as explained in Basic tutorial 5). As you know, the methodology to create flat drawings uses a Shape and a Detail layer. Quite often, when you start drawing details, they are open shapes, which Illustrator by default will fill with white. This can be problematic, because the white fill can cover the shape or other details. To compound the problem, the fact that every object created has a white fill makes it impossible to see why some objects are mysteriously disappearing. I have had had so many students asking me the same question over and over again: 'Why has my detail disappeared?' The best way to overcome this is by colouring the shape in a light non-obtrusive colour, such as a light grey. This will enable you to see if your details have a white fill.

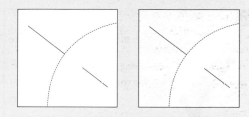

same open segment detail with a white fill viewed with two different background colours

Designing the details

For this classic shirt, you will design standard detailing, but feel free to experiment with more creative details. Let's start with the most important detail in a classic shirt, which is the collar.

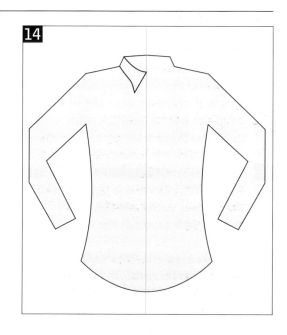

For the collar topstitch you will, for the first time, use the outline stroke technique to create a perfect parallel curve line:

13 Create a new layer and name it 'Details'; lock the Shape layer.

14 With the Pen tool (P), draw the left collar, using five anchor points, starting with the side collar point and then going to the collar CF (create Bezier curve here). Next is the collar tip, followed by the collar shape curve and finally the side neck point (Bezier curve). Click away.

15 Make sure your collar has no fill colour. Select the white arrow (A) and with it press and drag over the following anchor points: collar tip and collar shape (you can also use the Direct Select Lasso tool).

70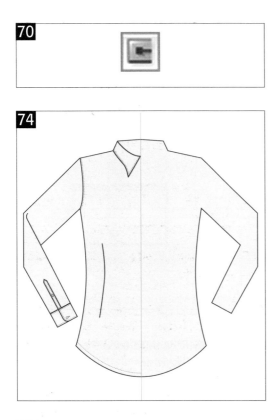

74

76

78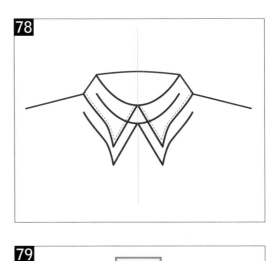

79

74 Select the Pen tool and use three anchor points to draw the front dart.

You can now mirror all the details you have created:

70 Paste in front (Command+F) and give the pasted segment a weight of 6pt and a Projecting Cap in the Stroke palette.

71 Go to Menu>Object>Path>Outline Stroke.

72 Select the Eyedropper tool (I) and click on the cuff topstitch line.

73 With the white arrow (A), select the unwanted anchor points and delete them with the backspace key.

75 Make sure the Shape layer is locked. With the black arrow, press and drag over all the details.

76 Select the Reflect tool (O) and mirror the details while pressing the Alt and Shift keys. Release the mouse button.

To draw the collar stand, use the collar fold curve, which will become the neckline:

77 With the black arrow, select both the left and right collars.

78 Press and drag them below to a new position where the neckline should be. Make sure you press Shift and Alt to constrain and duplicate. Release the mouse button.

79 Select the Scissors tool (C) and click on both duplicated collar fold lines where they join with the original collar. This will cut both segments in two distinctive parts.

80 Select the white arrow (A) and use it to pick both segments lying inside the collar. Press Backspace to delete them.

81 Select the direct select lasso (Q) and use it to lasso all the unwanted anchor points on both sides of the duplicated collar. Press Backspace to delete them.

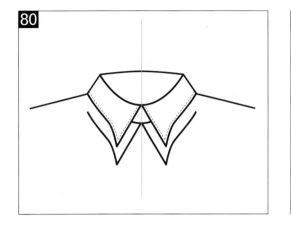

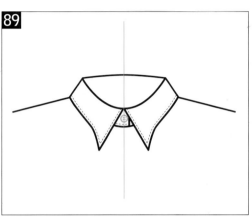

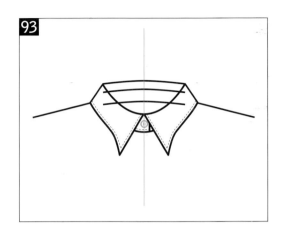

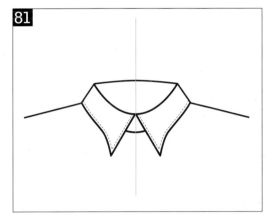

80

81

82   The remaining segment is your CF neckline, which needs to have its CF anchor points averaged and joined (Command+Alt+J and Command+J).

83   Select the newly created CF neckline with the black arrow (V); copy and paste it in front.

84   Give the pasted segment a weight of 3pt in the Stroke palette.

85   Go to Menu>Object>Path>Outline Stroke.

86   Select the Eyedropper tool (I) and click on the collar topstitch line.

87   With the white arrow (A), select the unwanted anchor points and delete them all with the backspace key.

88   Copy and paste the button from the cuff and move it to the CF neckline. Resize it if necessary. The button is grouped with the whole cuff so, to extract it, change to outline view (Command+Y) and, with the direct select lasso (Q), select the button and copy paste it.

89   With the Pen tool, draw a straight line made of two anchor points where the under collar opening should be.

To finish the under collar you need to draw the inside neck:

90   Unlock the Shape layer and select it. With the white arrow (A), select the CB neck anchor point by clicking on it.

91   Copy it. Next, lock the Shape layer and select the Details layer. In the layer palette option, make sure that Paste Remembers Layers is un-ticked.

92   Paste in front (Command+F) and, with the black arrow (V), move the CB neck down to where the top edge of the under collar should be. (Remember to press Shift and Alt to constrain and duplicate.)

93   Repeat this again to place the lower edge of the collar stand.

94   Select the Scissors tool (C) and use it to cut away the excess segments on the two lines just created.

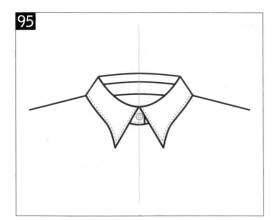

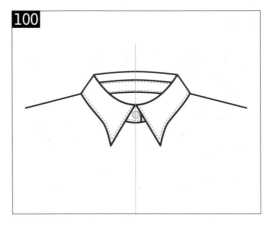

95 With the white arrow, select the unwanted segments and delete them with Backspace. (Make sure you press the Backspace key twice to delete the segment and then the stray anchor points).

96 Select the black arrow and pick the two segments. Copy and paste them in front.

97 In the Stroke palette, select a weight of 2pt.

98 Go to Menu>Object>Path>Outline Stroke.

99 Select the Eyedropper tool (I) and click on the collar topstitch line to clone it.

100 With the white arrow (A), select the unwanted anchor points and delete them with the backspace key.

The front view is finished by drawing the button stand:

101 Select the Rectangle tool (M), press and drag to create the button stand shape. Make sure it is centred and aligned with the collar stand opening (press Alt to grow your rectangle from the centre). Give your collar stand the same fill colour as the shape (use the Eyedropper tool for this).

102 Copy and paste in front the collar stand, giving it a stroke weight of 2pt and no fill colour.

103 Go to Menu>Object>Path>Outline Stroke.

104 Select the Eyedropper tool (I) and click on the collar topstitch line to clone it.

105 With the white arrow (A), select the unwanted anchor points and delete them with the backspace key.

And the front buttons:

106 With the black arrow (V) select the button on the collar stand. Bring it to front, go to >Menu>Object>Arrange> Bring to Front (or Command+Shift+])

107 Press and drag the button down towards the button stand, press Shift to constrain and Alt to duplicate.

108 Press Command+D to duplicate your move; this will create a new button, below the last one and at exactly the same distance.

109 Repeat this until your buttons reach the hem, or until you have enough buttons for your design.

110 If you want to change the distance between the buttons, simply move the last one closer to the one above it (you can bring it at close as you want.) Select all the buttons then go to the Align palette. In the Align palette pop-up option menu, select Show option and then click on Vertical Distribute Space under Distribute Spacing.

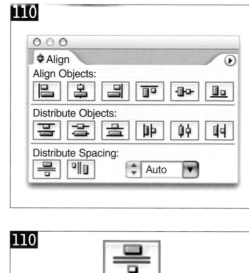

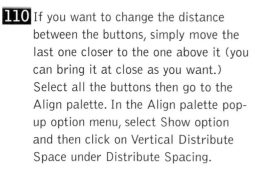

The back view

Start by duplicating the front shape and all details:

1   Unlock the shape layer and select all the shapes and details (Command+A).

2   With the black arrow (V), press and drag the whole shirt towards the lower right, then press Alt to duplicate and Shift to constrain at a 45-degree angle.

3   Press and drag a guide line for the back view.

4   Lock the Shape layer.

5   With the black arrow (V), pick the button stand and buttons, both sides of the collar and the top edge of the collar stand; press Backspace to delete them all.

6   Select the white arrow (A) and press and drag to select both anchor points on the left edge of the back neckline, then drag them towards the outer edge of the collar shape outline. Repeat for the right side. This will transform your back neck into the back collar.

7   With the black arrow (V), select the left sleeve fold detail. Select the Reflect

tool (O) and move the reflect target on the anchor point, touching the inside sleeve fold. Mirror the shape freely, without copying it, until it fits the back view fold.

8   You will need to shorten the fold detail so that it fits within the sleeve.

9   For the right side, simply delete the right sleeve fold detail and mirror and duplicate the left one.

10   We now need to delete the unwanted elements on the cuff (the cuff opening, the button and the whole placket). Simply do this with the white arrow and backspace key. You will need to extend the cuff hem topstitch after having deleted the cuff opening.

11   Now mirror the modified cuff to the right side.

The shirt is now finished! You can retouch it with extra details and maybe a thicker outline stroke. Note that if you wish to make the cuff outline thicker, you will need to ungroup the cuff (Command+Shift+G).

Chapter 9
Jacket Sketch Tutorial

The jacket you will create is a classic men's suit jacket. Since this is our fifth technical drawing and a suit jacket is quite similar to a shirt, we will go through the motions swiftly, only giving detailed instructions when a new skill is to be learned. In this chapter, you will find out how to design the collar of a suit jacket, visualize the lining details, create rounded pocket flaps swiftly and draw a keyhole buttonhole.

When you look at a suit jacket on a hanger or lying flat, the sleeves are usually covering the body sides. For our flat drawing, we will need to cheat a bit and tilt the sleeve slightly outwards, so the body shape can be made visible.

Designing the shape

A suit jacket shape is quite tricky to do in one go, so you might need to draw it a few times before you get what you want. A good way of doing this is to draw your first shape and, if you are not entirely happy with it, transform the shape into a guide (see below). Do this by selecting your shape with the black arrow and then Command+5 or Menu>View>Guides> Make Guides. This will help you draw your second shape, either following the guide line or creating new lines where there was a problem with the first draft. You can also use the dummy to help you keep the suit jacket proportions correct:

Transform a shape into a guide

1 Create a new A4 portrait document. Drag a ruler guide for the CF in the centre of the A4 page. Name the first layer 'Shape'.

2 With the Pen tool (P), draw half a shape, starting from the CF guide line and using a total of 13 anchor points: CB collar, neck side, collar side, shoulder, elbow, outer cuff, inner cuff, underarm, waist, side hem, middle hem, hem curve and finally CB hem.

3 The following anchor points should have Bezier curves: elbow, outer cuff, inner cuff, underarm, waist, side hem and hem curve; all the other anchor points have no curves.

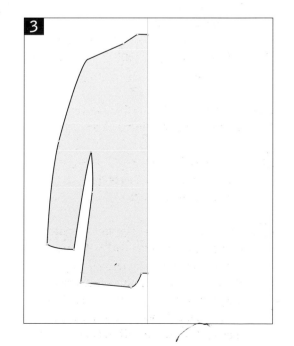

4 Adjust your shape with the white arrow (A), if necessary, or use the guide technique as explained above.

5 Select the entire shape with the black arrow (V).

6 Select the Reflect tool (O), move the reflect target to the CF line and mirror the shape.

7 Press Alt and Shift to duplicate and constrain. Release the Alt and Shift keys and then the mouse button.

8 With the white arrow (A), select the two CB collar end anchor points.

9 Average (Command+Alt+J) and then join (Command+J) the two end anchor points. Repeat this for the two other end anchor points (CB hem).

10 Your shape should now be one single object.

11 With the black arrow (V), you can select the shape and then use the bounding box to change its proportions, if necessary.

12 With the white arrow, select the CB collar point and transform it to a Bezier curve with the Convert Anchor Point tool (Shift+C). Making sure you hold down the Shift key to constrain the curve horizontally.

13 Fill the shape with a light grey colour.

Designing the details

One of the most important details in a suit jacket is the line comprising the neckline, lapels, front opening and hem shape. Usually this distinguishes the jacket's style and category (single breasted, double breasted and so on). Remember to make sure that none of the elements you will create for the details have a fill colour.

Let's start by designing the CF neck and front opening line:

14 Lock the Shape layer, create a new layer and name it 'Details'. Select the Pen tool (P).

15 Above the neck side anchor point, place your first anchor point for the CF neckline. Next, position the second one further below and a third one about where your lapel will end, making sure this anchor point is placed to the right of the CF line and far enough from it to allow buttons to be placed later. Your fourth and final anchor point should be right above the hem curve anchor point in the Shape layer. Click away.

16 To create a satisfying front opening line, you will need to retouch your anchor points and curves with the white arrow (A).

17

20

24

17 Note that all the anchor points, apart from the first one, have a Bezier curve.

Now let's create the collar and lapel:

18 With the Pen tool still selected, place an anchor point above the collar side; move below to place a second anchor point for the collar tip and a third one where the collar will meet with the lapel. Click away.

19 Place your first anchor point for the lapel above the front opening line and a second one to the left to create you top lapel segment. The third one should be placed where the lapel finishes into the front opening line. Click away.

20 With the white arrow (A), retouch your collar and lapel.

■ Quick tip

When you create a new segment by placing an anchor point above another segment in the same layer (as we have done for the collar and lapel), make sure that the other segment is not selected. If it is, your Pen tool will become an Add Anchor Point tool, so instead of creating a new segment you will add an anchor point to the other segment.

Now let's draw all the cut details (shoulder, armhole, darts and side panel):

21 With the Pen tool (P), draw the shoulder seam with two anchor points (no curve here). Click away.

22 Draw the armhole curve with three anchor points, making the second and third with Bezier curves. Make sure that the curve flows into the sleeve seamlessly, without any bumps. Click away.

23 Draw the side panel, either from scratch, with three anchor points, or by copy pasting in front the shape side segment (you only need to select the waist anchor point and make sure Paste Remembers Layers is un-ticked). Click away.

24 Finally, draw the front dart with two or three anchor points, depending on the shape you want to give it.

You are now going to draw the **front pocket**, which is a classic double-welted pocket with

Rounded Rectangle tool

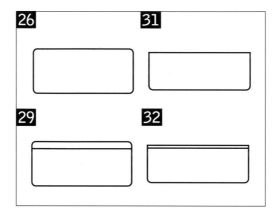

Knife tool

a rounded corner flap. The best way to draw
a round corner is to use the Rounded
Rectangle tool. Our pocket only needs two
round corners on the lower edge. We will use
the Knife tool to cut away the other rounded
corners. This technique is much faster than
drawing the flap from scratch.

25   Select the Rounded Rectangle tool (no
keyboard short cut). With it, press
and drag in a free space, next to the
jacket, to create your pocket flap.
Try to keep its size in proportion to
the jacket.

26   If the rounded corners are too big or
too small, simply single click on the art
board to create a new rounded
rectangle. This time you will see a
dialog box where you can input the
round corner value. (Leave the width
and height untouched; Illustrator by
default will have the same values as
your previously created rectangle.)

27   If necessary, delete the first rectangle.

28   Select the rectangle with the black
arrow (V).

29   Select the Knife tool (no keyboard
shortcut), which is found in the
embedded scissors palette.

30   Place your knife outside the rectangle,
on the left side just below the rounded
corner. Hold the Alt and Shift keys
down and then press and drag the Knife
tool across the rectangle, making sure
you go beyond the rectangle's right
edge. Release the mouse button and
then the Alt and Shift keys. Click away.

31   Select the black arrow (V), click on the
top part of the pocket and then press
backspace to delete it.

32   Repeat from steps 28 to 29 to create
the pocket jet. Use the black arrow (V)
to select the jet and the pocket flap
and group them (Command+G).

33   Your pocket is now ready. Simply press
and drag, while holding the Alt key, to
duplicate it to its final position.

34   Rotate and scale your pocket in
position, using the black arrow and, if
necessary, the bounding box. Give the

pocket the same light grey colour fill as
the shape so that it will cover the side
panel curve and match the shape colour.

You can now mirror the details:

35   Select all the details with the black
arrow. With the Reflect tool (O) mirror
the details, using the CF line as reflect
target and holding the Alt and Shift keys
to constrain and duplicate the details.

The next step is to get rid of the front
opening overlapping segment, in this case the
left side (or the right side if you are
designing a woman's jacket). Use the
Scissors tool to cut the unwanted segments:

36   Use the black arrow to select the left
front opening segment.

35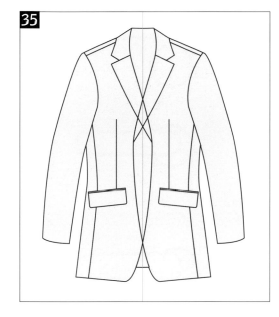

41

44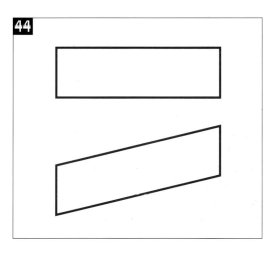

46

37 With the Scissors tool (C), click on the selected segment where it intersects the CF line and the right front opening segment (where the neckline crosses over).

38 Click a second time where the selected segment intersects the CF line and the right front opening segment again (where the hem curve crosses over).

39 With the white arrow (A), select the unwanted segments and then press backspace twice to delete them.

40 Select the left lapel segment with the black arrow (V). With the Scissors tool (C), click on it where it intersects with the right front opening segment.

41 Select the white arrow (A) again and click on the unwanted lapel segment. Press backspace to delete it.

Finish designing all the remaining front details, starting with the chest pocket:

42 Select the Rectangle tool (M), press and drag on the art board, next to the jacket, to create your chest pocket welt shape.

43 Select the Shear tool (no keyboard shortcut),which is embedded with the Scale tool.

43

44 Press and drag upwards while holding the Shift key down to constrain to a vertical shear.

45 Release the mouse and then the Shift key.

Back view

Let's start by duplicating the entire front shape and the details we need for the back view:

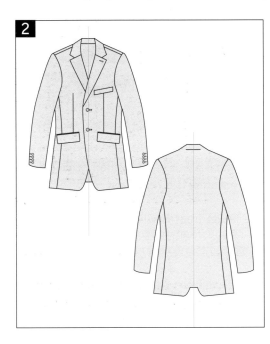

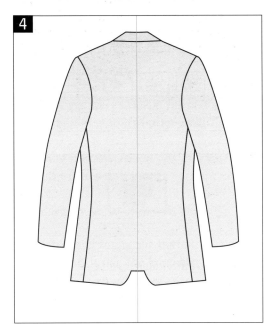

1 Unlock the Shape layer and select the shape, the two side panel lines and the CB neckline, using the black arrow (V).

2 Press and drag the shape and selected details towards the lower right, while pressing Alt to duplicate and Shift to constrain at a 45-degree angle.

3 Lock the Shape layer. Select the Detail layer.

4 With the white arrow (A) and the arrow keys, move the two end anchor points on the CB neckline so that they reach the neck sides.

5 Unlock the Shape layer and select it. Drop a horizontal guide line at the same height as the CB hem line.

6 With the black arrow (V), select the shape.

7 Select the Knife tool; go to the left and the outside of the back view shape, right on top of the new guide. Press and drag the Knife tool toward the right while holding down the Shift and Alt keys.

8 Go beyond the right of the shape; release the mouse and then the Shift and Alt keys.

9 With the black arrow, select the lower part of the back view and delete it with the Backspace key.

10 Lock the Shape layer. Select the black arrow and, in the Detail layer, select one side panel cut line.

Inside v

To finish this
illustrate the

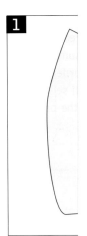

1

Instead of ex
create this ir
the key stage
images show
Remember tl
inside view d
factories usu
eventual insi

1 Recycl
details
will ne
and joi
shape

2 Recycl
detail
back v
some

8

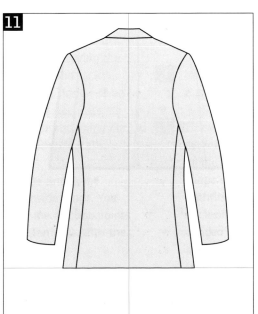

11

■ Quick tip

When you work with certain tools, such as the
Knife tool, you need great precision to perform
an action. To have a more precise cursor, press
the Caps Lock key (above the Shift key) and
your Knife tool will change from this to this.

11 Select the Scissors tool (C) and click
on the side panel cut line, where it
intersects the new hemline, deleting the
unwanted segment. Repeat this with
the other side panel cut line.

You will now put the finishing touches to the
back view by adding the **elbow cut line** in
the sleeve and a **CB cut line with a vent** in
the back:

12 Unlock the Shape layer again and
select the elbow anchor point with the
white arrow. Copy it and lock the
Shape layer. Paste it in front in the
Detail layer. Move the new segment
with the black arrow, taking it towards
the centre of your sleeve (using Shift to
constrain on a horizontal line).

13 Select the Scissors tool (C) and cut off
the unwanted segments.

14 Mirror and duplicate the elbow cut line
to the right sleeve.

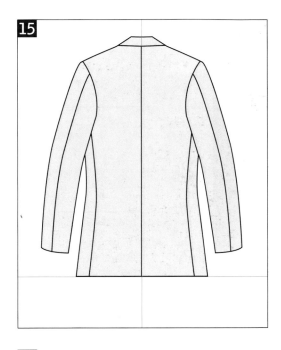

15

15 Using the Pen tool, draw the CB cut
line, using two anchor points and the
Shift key to constrain.

To represent the vent, we will use a **shading
technique,** which shows an opening where
the vent is located, even though there are no
design details to visualize this:

16 With the Pen tool (P) and on the CB
cut line, place an anchor point where
the vent should start. Go to the CB
hem and, while pressing Shift, place a
second anchor point. Finish with a
third and last anchor point to the right
along the hemline, only a few
millimetres away from the CB line.
Click away.

17

17 Give
grey
used

Your jack
it with ex
outline st

21

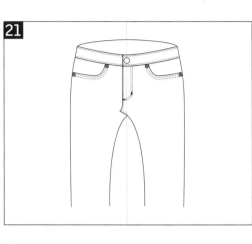

22–24

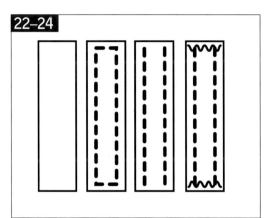

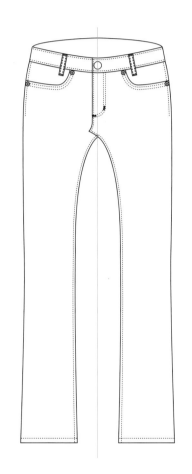

as with the waistband to create the parallel topstitch line. Use the Eyedropper tool to clone the topstitch from the waistband stitching.

20 With the Pen tool, draw the fly topstitch, using three anchor points and giving the segment a stroke weight of approximately 3pt. Outline Stroke it and use the Eyedropper tool to clone the topstitch from the waistband. Get rid of the superfluous lines at the top and bottom of the twin needle stitching with the white arrow. Adjust the lines if necessary.

21 Finish the fly front by drawing two bar tacks (refer to the Trousers tutorial for more details), using the Zig Zag filter.

The next items to design on the front are the belt loops:

22 In a free space on the art board, and with the Rectangle tool (M), draw a

belt loop, giving it the required proportions (make sure it has a fill colour). When the first rectangle is done, use the Scale tool (S) to resize the rectangle into a twin-needle topstitch, holding the Alt key to duplicate. Release the mouse button. Give this new rectangle no fill.

23 With the Eyedropper tool (I), clone a nearby topstitch and then use the white arrow (A) to select both the top and bottom segments of the topstitch. Cut and paste them in front (Command+F). In the Stroke palette, un-tick the dashed line box, and give both the pasted lines a stroke of 0.5pt.

24 Finally, transform these two segments into bar-tacks, using the Zig Zag filter. Finish off by grouping the belt loop with the bar-tack and topstitching.

You can now place your belt loops on the front view and finish with the remaining details, such as the hem, the hip and inner leg topstitching, using the techniques you have just learned.

Quick tip

Leave the inside view of the back waistband for later, when you are working on the back. This is a much faster way to work it out.

The back view

The back pocket and the topstitch wings (originally created by Levi and representing the Californian Eagle) is one of the key details on a pair of jeans. To create the pocket topstitch, we will use the new Align Stroke feature in Illustrator CS2, which is very useful to offset stroke lines. Unfortunately the feature is limited to closed shapes (which is why we did not use it for the topstitching on the front details, since they were open segments).

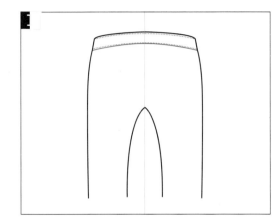

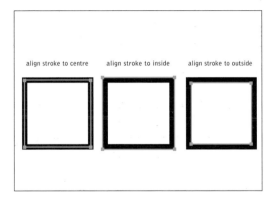

CS2 align stroke options

Let's start by designing the back waistband, CB line and the yoke:

1 Use the Pen tool to draw the back waistband, using the same Outline Stroke technique as for the front waistband.

2 Draw the CB line and topstitch with a single straight line, which you will then duplicate twice for the twin-needle topstitch. You can also release the Shape layer momentarily and select all the anchor points on the back crotch to nudge them down a few millimetres, since the CB is usually longer than the CF line.

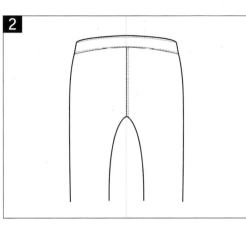

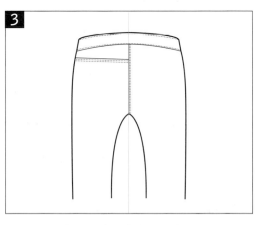

3 With the Pen tool, draw the yoke line and two topstitch lines, just as you have done with the CB line.

We will now move to the **back pocket design** using the new Align Stroke feature in Illustrator CS2. This enables you to move the stroke line to the right or left of the source segment, which is very useful for topstitch lines. If you do not work on CS2, create the topstitching in the same way as for the front pocket (from step 3):

4 Using the Rectangle tool (M), draw a shape representing your rough back pocket outline. Go to Menu>Object> Path>Add Anchor Points. With the Delete Anchor Point Pen tool, delete all added anchor points you do not need (all except the one located in the

4

5

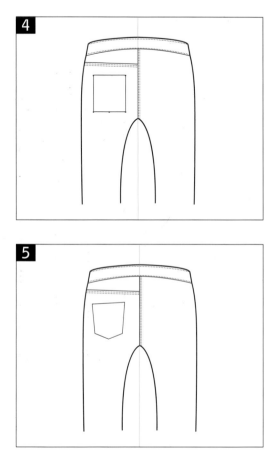

middle of your rectangle's lower
segment).

5 With the white arrow, nudge your
anchor points to shape the pocket.

6 Select the pocket with the black arrow
and then copy and paste it in front twice.
Give your second pasted pocket a stroke
weight of 3pt and, in the Stroke palette
(Illustrator CS2 only), tick the Align
Stroke to Inside icon under Align Stroke.

6

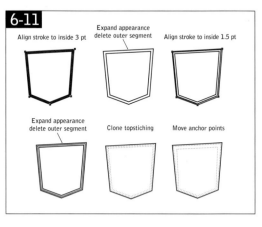

6

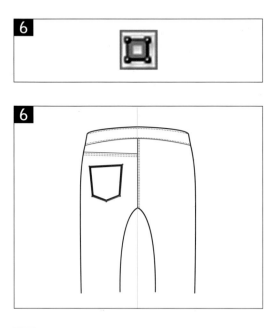

7 Go to Menu>Object>Expand
Appearance. Then, in the Tool palette,
click on the Swap Fill & Stroke arrow.
This creates two segment lines. Using
the white arrow, delete the outer
segment (the one lying on top of the
pocket line) entirely.

8 Select the first pasted outer segment
and give it a stroke of 1.5pt; in the
Stroke palette (Illustrator CS2 only),
tick the Align Stroke to Inside icon
under Align Stroke.

9 Go to Menu>Object>Expand Appearance.
Then in the Tool palette click on the
Swap Fill & Stroke arrow. This creates
two segment lines. Use the white arrow
to delete the outer segment (the one
lying on top of the pocket line) entirely.

6-11
Align stroke to inside 3 pt   Expand appearance delete outer segment   Align stroke to inside 1.5 pt

Expand appearance delete outer segment   Clone topstiching   Move anchor points

11

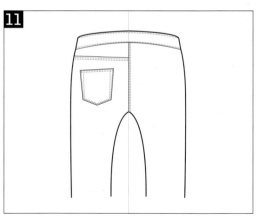

10 Give the two inner segments a
topstitch, using the Eyedropper tool.

11 With the white arrow, select and move
the relevant anchor points on the inner
topstitch line to get a more realistic
denim pocket look and feel.

12 Draw the pocket wing with the Pen
tool; give it a generous stroke weight
then stroke outline it. Finish by giving
the wing a topstitch.

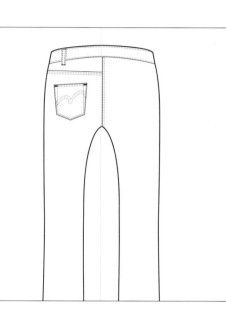

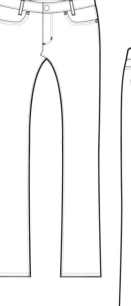

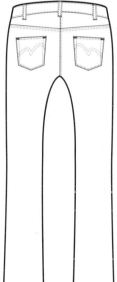

13 Finish the pocket by creating a couple of bar-tacks on the top corners.

To finish the back view, you only need to add the belts loops and hem topstitches:

14 Select the belt loop created for the front view and drop it into the back waistband, on the left side only.

15 Draw the hem topstitch line on the left side only.

16 Mirror, constrain and duplicate all the details to the right side, except for the CB line and the waistband.

17 Add the centre CB belt loop.

18 Finish by duplicating the back waistband onto the front; scissor and delete the overlapping segments.

Your jeans are now completed, but you can retouch and adjust any details, if necessary.

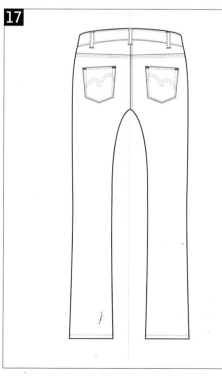

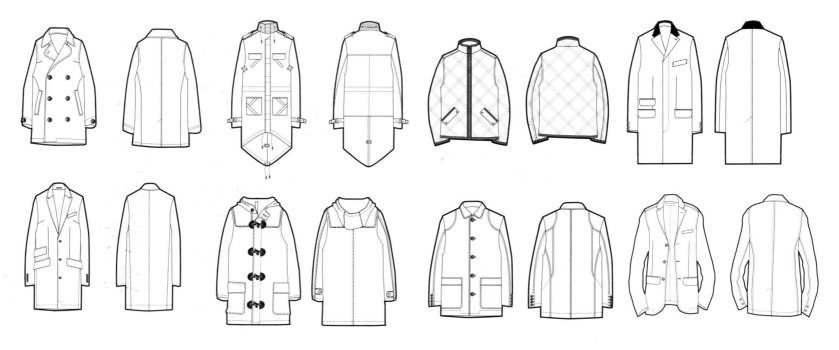

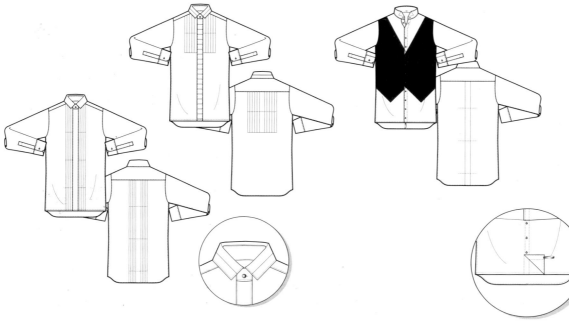

Lukas
These flats have a very professional look, and strike a perfect balance between factory specs and sale/ promotional catalogue material.

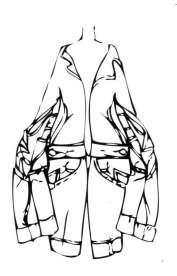

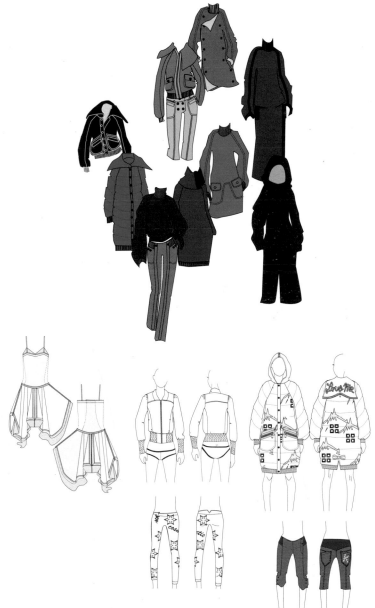

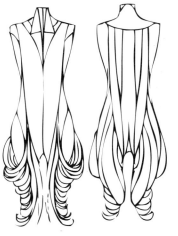

Alithia Spuri Zampetti

These garment sketches were made using the Live Trace features in Illustrator CS2. Alithia sketched all the garment flats by hand and scanned them before applying a custom setting in Live Trace options, which suited the drawing style best.

Binia Umland

Very creative garment rendering with great use of the dummy, which gives the flats a better sense of proportion. The top drawings show a great use of Illustrator's distortion tools, giving the flats an enhanced dynamic and flowing effect.

Chapter 13
Knitwear and Geometric Patterns

Now that you have mastered the creation of various garment sketches, it is time to look at more advanced and specialized design skills. Over the next six chapters you will learn new skills that go beyond simple garment flat drawings. The advanced skills chapters have two sections: the first section deals with advanced flat drawing visualization, and this is followed by the advanced details design section. Advanced flat drawing visualization looks into Illustrator's capabilities to visualize a garment sketch more realistically and in more detail. A more accurate rendering of the garment flat drawing is very useful when designers want to communicate their creation beyond the classic factory and production environment. The ever-increasing yearly collection output means that quite often a company will have to sell new designs on paper without having the final sales samples ready for clients. This is where visualizing garments as closely as possible to the real thing becomes very useful. Over the first three advanced skills chapters we will look at how to create geometric patterns and complex all-over prints; how to import and visualize real fabric samples into a garment shape with added wash effects and, finally, how to visualize placement prints artworks onto garments. In the second part of the advanced skills chapters, you will learn how to create realistic and complicated detailing, including advanced trim designs and a trims library, using brushes and styles for detailing and visualization and, finally, how to brand trims and create fashion graphics.

In the last basic shape tutorial, you learned how to create a simple two-tone stripe design. This was the beginner's level introduction to Illustrator's powerful Pattern Swatch tool. You will now learn a more advanced technique with which to create geometric swatch patterns. Knitwear has been selected to represent geometric patterns, but the same technique can be applied for any type of geometric pattern, such as tweeds, ginghams, checks and so on. This chapter does not deal with specific knitwear design issues, such as gauges, yarns knitting technique and the like. It is solely dedicated to visualizing a knitwear pattern or any other geometric shape.

The main difficulty with rendering geometric patterns is the repeat sequence process. As you already know, Illustrator 'tiles' a pattern swatch inside any shape fill. Making the tiling process seamless can be tricky; only trial and error and patience will help you create a perfect geometric swatch pattern with seamless tiling.

Designing a Knitwear Garment

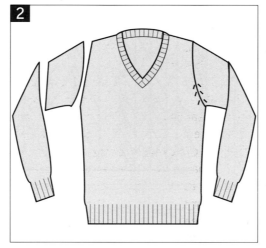

Let's get started by designing a knitwear garment shape:

1 Copy the knitwear shape pictured, with a half front containing 15 anchor points. Alternatively, and even better, create your own garment, making sure that there is a minimum of two layers (Shape and Detail). To keep the focus on creating a knitwear pattern swatch, we will only work on the front view.

2 Divide the sleeves in two separate objects, using the armhole and sleeve fold as dividing paths. This is the same technique as explained in chapter 11, under 'divide a shape'. Refer to the chapter if you have trouble getting the right result.

3 The rib design is usually important for knitwear shapes (refer to chapter 11: 'creating ribs' to see how to do this). You can achieve many different kinds of rib design by varying the line weight, dash and gap. In the sketch pictured, for example, the rib has a weight of 33pt, a dash of 0.5pt and a gap of 7pt.

■ Quick tip

You can also use the Brush tool to create ribs. The Stroke palette can produce unsatisfactory ribs when dealing with certain curves, whereas brushes are more accurate for curved ribs. Go to chapter 17 to learn how to use brushes for ribbing.

Now that your shape is ready, you can start the process of **creating a geometric knit pattern swatch**:

4 Make sure the rulers are visible (Command+R). Drag a vertical and horizontal ruler in a free space next to your knitwear shape (creating a simple cross guide).

5 Select the Rounded Rectangle tool and draw a shape like the one pictured. Make sure it has a white fill and then use the Shear tool to skew the shape (pressing Shift to constrain) to roughly 45 degrees.

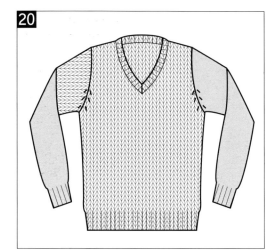

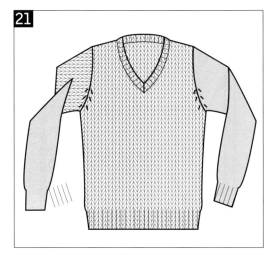

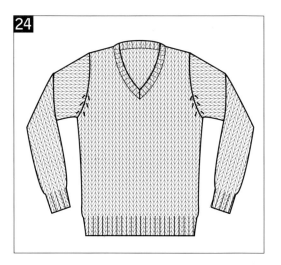

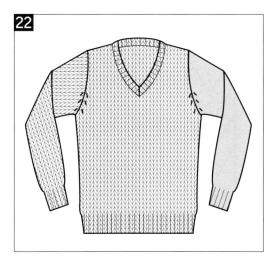

tutorial. First, make sure that your preferences setting has a ticked box under Transform Pattern Tiles.

20 Select one top sleeve with the black arrow and rotate the sleeve (pressing Shift to constrain) by 90 degrees (either way). Fill the sleeve with the knit pattern, then rotate the sleeve back to its original position. The pattern now has the correct grain line.

21 For the forearm, use the same technique, but this time rotate it until the sleeve hem is perfectly horizontal.

22 Fill the forearm with the pattern swatch and rotate it back into position.

23 To fill in the other top sleeve, use the Eyedropper tool. To fill in the other forearm, repeat steps 21 and 22.

24 Finish your jumper by making the rib thicker if it is concealed by the knit pattern.

You can use this technique for unlimited types of geometric pattern. The technique to create them will always be the same.

■ Quick tip

You can use any drawing tool to draw a geometric pattern swatch (Pen tool, Pencil, Rectangle, Ellipse, Star tool, and so on), but make sure it is not coloured with gradients, blends, brush strokes, meshes, bitmap images or placed files.

Chapter 14
All-over Print Patterns

All-over print patterns tend to contain organic shapes, set in a structured repeating sequence over the print area. Because the shapes tend to be laid over a less rigid geometric grid than other patterns, it is usually harder to spot the repeat. A good all-over print should look and feel like a single piece of artwork. This tutorial looks at three different types of all-over print. We start with prints made of randomly placed objects, followed by prints containing organic shapes laid over a more structured repeat sequence and then, finally, prints containing continuous and organic artwork lines, which need to be seamlessly connected to create a flowing repeat effect.

Random Print Patterns

For this random object repeat print, you will need to create a floral design from scratch. Drawing real-life shapes in Illustrator without a template can be quite hard, so use research pictures to trace them with the Pen tool.

1 Find or take pictures of any organic object you fancy, either with your digital camera, mobile phone, scanner, on the web or in a good old-fashioned book. Make sure your images are not too big in file size (A6 size at 150dpi max), to avoid Illustrator's performance slowing down dramatically.

2 Create a new document and place your selected pictures by going to Menu>File>Place. When all your pictures are placed, lock the layer.

3 Create a new layer and use the Pen tool to trace over the pictures in order to create your objects. (Make sure your path has no fill to avoid concealing your pictures.)

4 Once you are finished with your objects, select them all and scale them, if necessary, to the size you want them for your print.

5 In a free space on your art board, draw a rectangle, which will become your pattern swatch area.

6 With the rectangle still selected, go to the Transform palette, and round up the rectangle's dimensions (for example W: 130mm H: 110mm). You can also use the Control palette in Illustrator 12.

7 Lock your rectangle so that it will not get in the way.

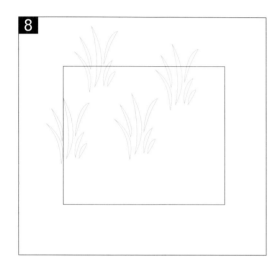

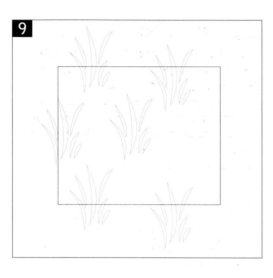

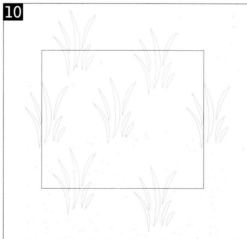

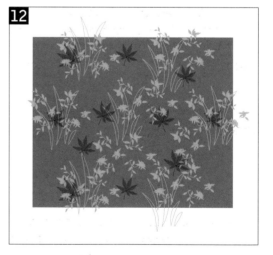

8 Select one of your traced objects and lay it out over the rectangle, but only either fully inside the rectangle or overlapping the rectangle's top and left edge. (It is important that you lay objects over the rectangle's edge if you are to create a seamless all over-print.)

You now need to move and copy the overlapping objects from the top edge to the bottom of the rectangle and from the left to the right edge **to create a seamless repeat.** This can be achieved easily and precisely with the Move tool:

9 Using the black arrow, select all the objects overlapping the rectangle's top edge. Go to Menu>Object>Transform>Move (Command+Shift+M) and input under Position: Horizontal: 0mm, Vertical: 110mm. Tick the preview box to check if the movement looks correct. Press Copy to confirm.

10 Select all the objects overlapping the rectangle's left edge and go to Menu>Object>Transform>Move. Input under Position Horizontal: 130mm, Vertical: 0mm and tick the preview box to check if the movement looks correct. Press Copy to confirm.

11 Lay your other objects over the rectangle's top and left edge and repeat step 1 and 10.

12 Unlock and give the rectangle a fill colour and no stroke, then copy it and send it to back (Command+Shift+[). Give the copied rectangle no fill and no

14

stroke. Make the coloured rectangle slightly bigger to avoid any tiling gaps.

13 Select both rectangles and all other objects. Drag and drop them into the Swatch palette.

14 Test the all-over print by filling it into a shape of your choice.

Remember that you can change the swatch size, colour and content easily, either by dragging and dropping it from the swatch palette or by reworking the original artwork and dropping it into the palette again.

■ **Quick tip**

For interesting visual effects, you can make some of your objects **translucent** by changing their opacity percentage or give them a different **blending mode.** Simply select any object and go to the Transparency palette to change the parameters (this works best when objects are overlapping and there is a background colour).

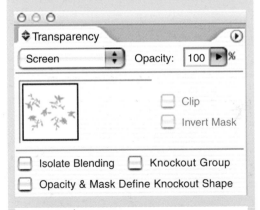

Leaf: blending mode: Exclusion Opacity 60%
Flower: blending mode: Screen
Grass: blending mode: Multiply

Organic shapes with structured repeat

Our second all-over print category, organic shapes with structured repeat, is closer to geometric patterns because it is based on a structured layout. This is where the comparison ends; a more organic shape content gives the print a less rigid look and feel than regular geometric prints. Creating structured repeats can be quite a daunting task and it is better to source a structured repeat print to use as a template for the repeat sequence. You can modify the print design on paper, either before you scan it in or as you trace the source print. It is important to observe the source print and understand how the repeat works out. You only need to trace the master element, which repeats itself over the print.

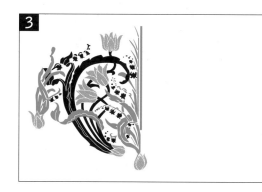

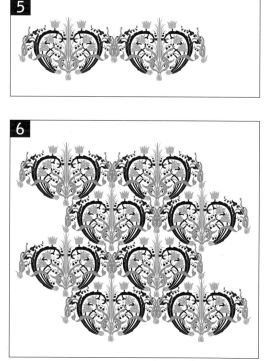

1   Create a new document and place your selected source print pictures (Menu>File>Place). Lock the layer.

2   Create a new layer and, using the Pen tool, trace over the master element, creating as many separate objects as required by the print. (Make sure your path has no fill to avoid concealing your source picture and use a stroke colour which is not similar to the colours in your source picture, for better visibility.)

3   When you're finished with the tracing, fill the various elements in the colours you want. Select all and group.

4   Mirror, constrain and duplicate your master element.

5   Group both sides into one; mirror, duplicate and constrain them again, if

necessary (depending on your repeat sequence).

6   Repeat until you have enough master elements to create a pattern swatch.

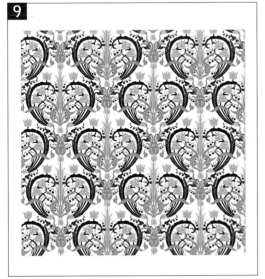

8 Press and drag a rectangle from the guide line to create your pattern swatch bounding box. Make sure it has no fill and no stroke colour. Send it to the back.

9 Select all and drop into the swatch palette. Verify your new pattern by filling it into a bigger rectangle than your original bounding box.

10 If desired, add a background colour to your print, just as you did in the previous all-over print tutorial. You can also alter your original artwork, varying the colours and sizes.

■ **Quick tip**

To make sure your print repeats itself well, try to include easy-to-spot reference points when you mirror the master element. In the print illustrated, the central green stalk is a simple segment line, which doubles up as a clear reference point for the mirroring target.

7 Place two vertical and two horizontal guide lines where you think the edges of the repeat sequence are.

Continuous and organic artwork lines

The third and final all-over print features continuous and organic artwork lines. Unlike the two other all-over prints, this one has seamlessly connected objects or lines to create a flowing repeat effect. For this print, you will learn how to work with Illustrator 12's powerful new feature: Live Trace.

As you might have noticed in the previous tutorials, manually tracing organic shapes can be quite tedious and take a lot of time. Live Trace enables you to do this automatically. The only drawback is that you will need to have a cleaned-up template image because, since Live Trace is automatic, anything that is on your template picture will be traced. Live Trace has many settings to choose from, depending on what kind of template picture you are working on. Preset elements, such as Photo High Fidelity, Black and White Logo, Hand Drawn Sketch and so on can help you get the best out of your template image tracing. It is nevertheless better to use Tracing Option to have more control over your tracing. For those of you who are not working with Illustrator CS2, you will have to trace the template picture manually, and can catch up the tutorial after the live tracing section. For this tutorial, I chose a template image that will need specific alterations to achieve a desired print. Your image might be totally different; if this is the case, go through the tutorial and adapt it to your own specific needs.

1   Select a template image containing continuous lines, such as a zebra or tiger print, camouflage or fingerprints.

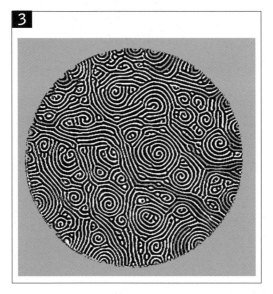

2   In Photoshop or any other picture-editing software, clean up your image so that it has as little noise, dust or scratches as possible. Your image should be around 150dpi for a size not exceeding A6 format.

3   In Illustrator CS2, open a new document and then go to Menu>File>Place and open your selected image.

4   Go to Menu>Objects>Live Trace>Tracing Option. In the tracing

option dialog box, tick on the preview box. Depending on your image content and style, you should select different modes to get the best tracing results. For the image used here, I selected strokes (no fills) and black and white setting. All the other settings were left unchanged.

5   In the Control palette, single click the Expand button.

6   If necessary, modify the stroke weight; for this artwork, I gave all strokes 1pt.

7   Ungroup the live traced object (Command+Shift+G). To give the print a more personal look and feel, you can add or delete some of the lines or even

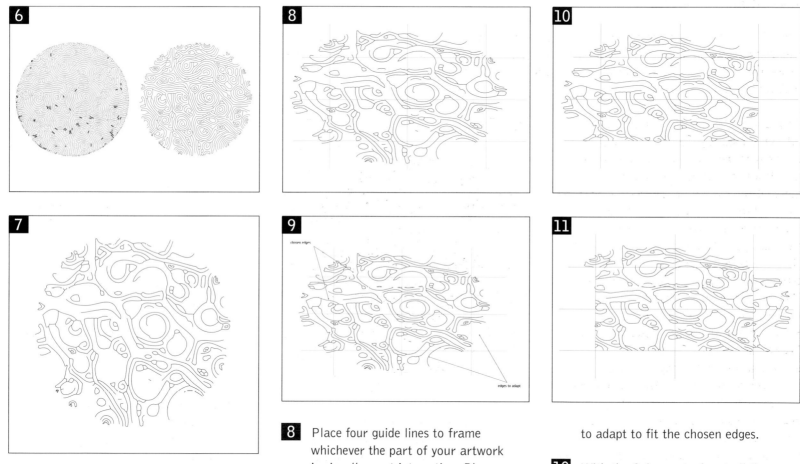

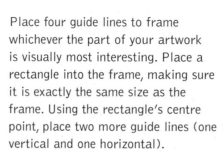

stretch the artwork. You can also use some type of filter, such as Roughen (Menu>Filter>Roughen), to give a more distinctive look to the print lines.

Your artwork is now ready to be **transformed into a seamless repeat pattern.** This is the most difficult part of continuous organic line patterns, because you will have to create or modify every line individually to make it fit into the repeat sequence.

8 Place four guide lines to frame whichever the part of your artwork is visually most interesting. Place a rectangle into the frame, making sure it is exactly the same size as the frame. Using the rectangle's centre point, place two more guide lines (one vertical and one horizontal).

9 Look at your artwork edges closely and choose which of the vertical and horizontal edges you want to use as a template for the seamless repeat and which one you will need

to adapt to fit the chosen edges.

10 With the Scissors tool, cut all the segments on all the edges, then delete the segments of both sides you will adapt to fit the chosen edges.

11 Using the black arrow, select all the elements outside the vertical chosen edge (the left one in this case). Mirror and constrain them to the right edge, using the frame centre line as a target (no need to duplicate).

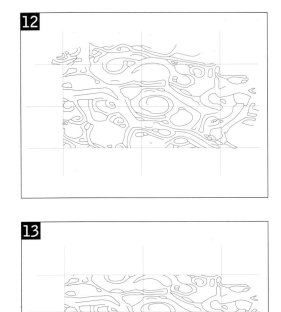

not, correct your original artwork and drop it again into the swatch palette, repeating this until you get the perfect seamless swatch.

You can use this print on any flat drawing you wish (this can be useful to check the print proportions).

12 With the white arrow, move the segments located inside the frame so that they connect with the one outside the frame edge. If you are missing some segments, use the Pen tool to draw new ones to match the mirrored ones. (Make sure you never alter the mirrored segments and that your segments on the inside on the frame go slightly beyond the frame edge to avoid any gaps.)

13 Repeat steps 11 and 12 on the horizontal edge.

14 Your artwork is now ready to be dropped in the Swatch palette, but before doing this, select the rectangle you created in step 1; give it no fill and no stroke and send it to the back. You can also copy it and paste it in back and then lock it and give the original rectangle a fill colour. This done, unlock the no fill, no stroke rectangle.

When you have dropped the artwork in the swatch palette, apply it to any shape to see if the seamless edges are working well. If

■ Quick tip

If you intend to produce any of your prints, you can always prepare your document for print factories. Simply create a new document with the same size as your print factory specifications (for example print on roll 160cm/64in wide by 70cm/28in). In the document, create a rectangle covering the whole art board area and fill it with your print swatch. You can resize your swatch to get the best repeat look and feel. This document will give you an idea of how your print will look in actual size and how often it will repeat on the whole fabric length.

Chapter 15
Fabrics, Wash Effects and Placement Prints

Another way to give your flat drawings a more realistic look is to fill them with fabric that has been scanned in an image editing software, such as Adobe Photoshop. On top of the fabric, you can also simulate a denim wash or jersey dye effect. If you work in the sportswear or casual wear industry, it is crucial to visualize placement prints and logos on your garments. This tutorial will cover all these techniques in detail and hopefully help you create a flat drawing looking as close to reality as possible.

Fabrics

Let's start with fabric placement. Basically, this works in the same way as placing any digital picture into Illustrator, but because we want our fabric to fit into a shape and pictures are rectangles, we will have to use the compound path technique to create an invisible mask to hide the unwanted bits of the picture. It is important to place a picture of fabric that is in proportion with the flat drawing. We will work with the Jeans flat drawing you created in chapter 10 (you can use any other flat drawing if you wish):

1 Open your Jeans flat drawing; unlock the Shape layer and hide the Detail layer.

2 Using the black arrow, select the shape, in the Transform palette or the Control palette (CS2 only). Write down the width and height measurements.

3 Scan in your selected denim fabric with an image editing software; try to have a denim swatch as close to A4 as possible.

4 Give your denim picture a file size equivalent to the measurement of your jeans shape. (For Photoshop, go to Menu>Image>Image Size.) Make sure you keep the proportions constrained, input the height value first and check that the width value is big enough to cover your shape.

5 Keep the image dpi size around 150 to 300 maximum (depending on your computer performance, 300 is best). Save your document as a Jpeg image.

6 Going back to your Illustrator document, select the Rectangle tool and draw a rectangle, framing the jeans front shape with a 2–3cm margin around it.

7 Select the front shape; copy and paste it in front and lock it (Command+2).

8 Select the rectangle and the original front shape and then go to Menu>Object>Compound Path>Make (or Command+8).

9 Give your compounded path a white fill and no stroke.

10 Create a new layer and name it 'Fabric'. Drag it to the bottom of your layer list.

11 Go to Menu>File>Place and select the denim fabric document. Place it under your compound path into the front shape view.

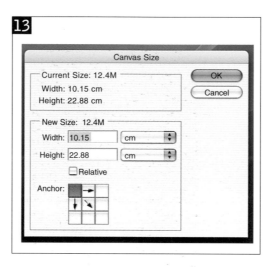

12 Check that the proportion of the denim weave to your shape is fine (avoid too big or too small weaves).

13 If the fabric is not at the right proportion, go back to Photoshop and change the file size as follows:

If the weave is too small, make the image size bigger and then crop it to the jeans shape dimensions.

If it is too big, make the image size smaller, then go to Menu>Image> Canvas Size. In the dialog box, give the canvas the same height and width as your shape. Make sure you tick on the top left arrow in the Anchor box.

14 You now have a big white space. This needs to be filled in with your denim fabric, located in the top-left corner; to do this, select the denim with the

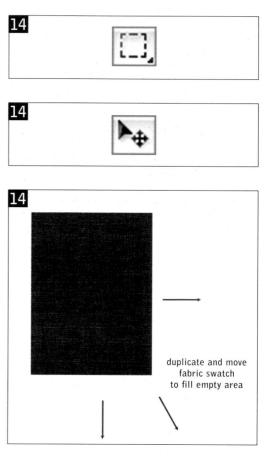

duplicate and move
fabric swatch
to fill empty area

rectangular Marquee tool. Copy and paste the fabric then select the Move tool. Move your fabric towards the gap. Paste again and move towards another gap. Repeat until your fabric covers the whole area.

15 Go to the Layer palette and select Flatten Image in the palette option pop-up menu. If you have scanned the fabric properly, you should not see any visible flaw lines where the different

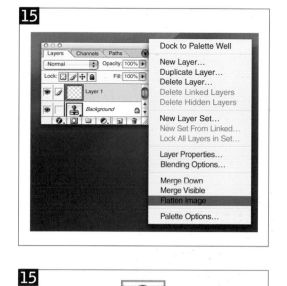

pieces of fabric overlap. If there are flaw lines, use the Clone Stamp tool to try to smooth out and erase them.

16   Save your fabric file as 'Denim small (or big) weave'. Then place it into Illustrator again. Having a big or small weave on the fabric alters your vizualization quite dramatically, as shown in the picture, right.

Wash effects

Your shape is now ready for the next operation, which is to visualize washing effects. At this stage, you can really let your imagination run wild and create any wash effects you can think of. The technique to create any kind of wash effects is the same, from denim engineered wash to jersey overdyes or any other distress, enzyme, sand, acid washes and so on. The main tool used to create a wash effect is the Paintbrush tool, used with transparency blending modes. The paintbrush is a very versatile tool and can be used in many different ways. Chapter 17 covers this in more detail, but for now you will work with the art paintbrush and brush libraries:

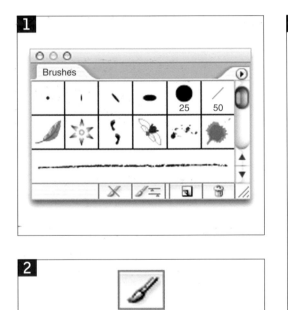

1 Go to Menu>Window>Brushes. You should see the paintbrush default library palette.

2 In the Tool palette, select the Paintbrush tool (B) and in the Brush palette select a brush style you fancy or go to Menu>Window>Brush Library (or brush palette pop up menu

option>brush libraries for CS2) and choose a brush library. (For the denim distress effect pictured, the Artistic Paintbrush library was used).

3 Create a new layer, called 'Wash', above the shape area. Lock all other layers.

4 Press and drag the Paintbrush tool to

create a brush stroke. Release the mouse button to finish the stroke.

5 Try to paint one leg, using various brushes.

6 Once painted, you can easily retouch the brush stroke by moving the anchor points around with the white arrow.

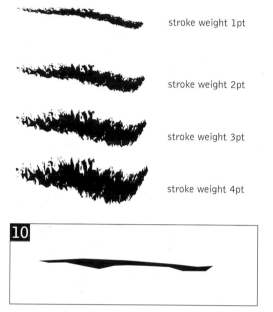

stroke weight 1pt

stroke weight 2pt

stroke weight 3pt

stroke weight 4pt

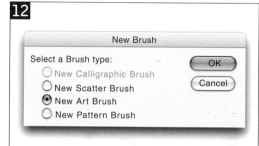

7 You can experiment with different brush styles by selecting your brush stroke with the black arrow and then applying any other brush in the brush palette.

At this stage the wash effect looks more like paint on jeans than anything else. **To give the brush stroke the correct look, use Illustrator's transparency or blending mode effects:**

8 When you are satisfied with the painted stroke on the jeans leg, select all your brush strokes.

9 Go to the Transparency palette and select a blending mode in the pop-up menu on the top-left corner. (Dodge

Colour Blending Mode works well for denim) and apply opacity to around 40 per cent.

You can also **make the brush stroke thinner or fatter** by changing its stroke weight.

If you're not happy with the brushes available, **you can create your own brush from scratch:**

10 In a free space on the art board, use the Pen tool or any other tool to create an object that will become your new brush style.

11 Select the object with the black arrow and drop it into the Brush palette (make sure that it is the main default brush palette).

12 In the new brush dialog box, select new art brush.

13 In the brush option simply press OK. (There are many options which are not relevant for now, but feel free to experiment.)

14 Select the Brush tool and paint with it, using your new brush style.

Once you are happy with the look of your wash effect on one leg, you can mirror it onto the other, but you might find that the effect looks different because brushes are often asymmetrical. If this is the case, try to draw the wash on the right leg from scratch or rotate rather than mirror the left leg wash.

asymmetrical leg   symmetrical leg

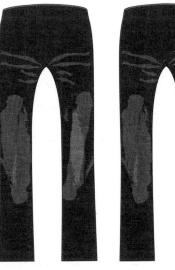 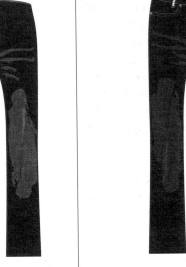

The next step is to **visualize the wash with the details layer:**

15 Make the Details layer visible.

16 Notice that the belt loops, the button and the rivets are filled with white.

17 Select the button and fill it in any colour you wish, such as a light grey, looking like silver. Do the same for the rivets.

18 Select the belt loops and ungroup them. Next, select the outer rectangle only and give it no fill.

19 Select all the elements of the belt loop; group them again and then lock them (Command+2).

20 Select the Scissors tool, and cut off the parts of the waistband that overlap the two belt loops.

21 Release the belt loops (Command+Alt+2).

To finish your jeans visualization, paint more wash effects, which can match the details. You can also play around with the blending modes and give your topstitching different colours. Have a look at the jeans pictured here, to inspire you.

For those of you not working with denim, use exactly the same techniques as described in this tutorial and adapt them for your style and garment type.

Placement prints

This section looks at how to display, in a shape, placement prints created in other applications, such as Adobe Photoshop. It does not cover the creation of placement prints, since most fashion companies employ graphic designers to produce the prints. Fashion designers tend to research for print and graphic mood boards and give art direction to the graphic team. Fashion designers can achieve much higher visual impact for their collection presentation if they include placement prints made for their flats, especially if they work in the casual and sportswear industry. When you place any image into a shape, it will always be in a rectangle and the image will stand out and fail to blend properly with the shape's fill colour (unless of course it is the same as that of the print). Illustrator's powerful transparency blending modes will again help to resolve this issue. Before you start the tutorials, remember that while Illustrator can place many different kinds of digital picture files, it can also struggle if the file sizes are too big (depending on your computer's performance). With this in mind, always keep the file size low by measuring the flat drawing and making sure that the digital file is about the same dimension and the dpi count is no bigger than 300.

1 Open the T-shirt tutorial flat drawing (or any other flat you choose). Select where you want to display the print: either the front or back shape. In the transform palette, write down the height and width measurements.

2 Apply a fill colour or pattern swatch to the selected shape.

3 Create a new layer, name it 'Mask' and place it between the shape and the detail layer. Create a compound path with the body shape if you think your print will overlap the shape area (go to the Fabrics tutorial to learn how to do this). If your shape contains more than one part (for example, a main body and two sleeves), the compound path you just created will cover sleeves. You will need to copy and paste these

3 compound path rectangle masking shape layer

3 shape layer sleeves cut & pasted into detail layer

into the detail layer above the mask
layer (see illustration).

4 In your image editing software, apply
the same dimensions to your artwork
as the selected shape and give it an
appropriate dpi size.

5 In Illustrator, create a new layer,
naming it 'Artwork' and placing it
between the Mask and Shape layers.

6 Go to Menu>File>Place and select
your artwork file. Place it onto the
shape as shown.

7 The placed print is masking the shape
stripe pattern. To change this, go to the
Transparency palette blending mode
pop-up menu and select Multiply

(which will knock off your artwork's
background colour). You can also
experiment with another blending mode
if you choose.

There are many possibilities and
variations for placement prints with
Illustrator, but they all work under the
same three basic rules: 1) make your
artwork image the same size as the flat
drawing and make sure the dpi count is
not greater than 300; 2) keep your
layers in order, from bottom to top:
Shape, Artwork, Mask, Details, and 3)
use the Transparency palette and its
blending modes to knock off the
artwork background.

Chapter 16
Advanced Trim Design and Trim Libraries

This second part of the Advanced Skills Tutorials looks at how to create both realistic and complex trim designs, as well as trim libraries. This is followed by techniques using brushes and styles for detailing and visualization and then by information on how to brand trims and create fashion graphics. Let's start with the trim design section.

Trims are not unfamiliar at this stage, since you have already created quite a few in the fashion sketch tutorials section. This chapter goes further into trim design without looking at garments themselves.

The best way to work efficiently when it comes to trims with Illustrator is to create documents dedicated solely to trims. These can then be made into trim libraries, which can be used for any garment sketches you are working on. Just as designers have libraries of trim suppliers' catalogues and samples which they would use to compose a trim selection for a collection, so you can create a trim library with Illustrator. In fact, you can create various libraries containing, for example, only zippers, cuff details or buttons and so on.

Trim libraries

Let's start by using the trims already designed in one of the previous tutorials. The best way to do this is to transform every single trim into Illustrator's symbols. Symbols are objects stored in the symbols palette and reusable on your document. Unlike pattern swatches, however, symbols can be dropped individually onto the artwork without having to be part of a shape or object. They remain independent and are therefore best suited for trims and design details. The best part is that you can create a symbol library very easily once you have dropped all your trims into the symbol palette.

A trim library is created as follows:

1. Open the denim sketch tutorial file.

2. Select and copy all the required trims (rivets, belt loops, pockets and so on) and paste them in a new document.

3. In the new document, go to Menu>Window>Symbols.

4. With the black arrow, select one denim trim or design detail and drag and drop it into the Symbols palette.

5. Repeat step 4 with all the design details and trims on your art board.

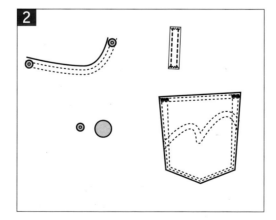

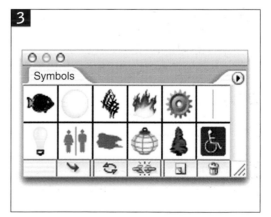

6. When you have all the required trims in the Symbols palette, you will need to delete all the unwanted symbols in the palette (these come as standard with Illustrator). Do so by selecting, one by one, all the unwanted symbols (press Shift to multiple select).

8

7   Go into the Symbols palette option pop-up menu and choose Delete symbol.

8   To avoid your library file size becoming too big, you should also delete in their respective palettes all unwanted colour swatches, styles and brushes. Do this by choosing Select All Unused on each palette's option pop-up menu. Then click the bin icon, on the lower right of the palette's window, to delete all unused elements.

9   Save the file as 'Denim trims and design details'.

10   Open a new document and go to Menu>Window>Symbol Libraries>Other Library. Find and select the denim trim file. (You can access the other symbols libraries directly in the Symbols palette option pop-up menu with Illustrator CS2.)

11   You should now see the denim trim Symbol library palette.

12   To use the symbols, simply drag them onto the art board.

Symbols are not editable beyond the bounding box scale and rotate. If you need to edit the anchor points, simply select the

11

denim trims library

Expand

Expand
☑ Object
☑ Fill
☐ Stroke

OK

Cancel

Expand Gradient To
◯ Gradient Mesh
◯ Specify: 255   Objects

symbol to edit on the art board and go to Menu>Object>Expand. In the dialog box, press OK. Your symbol is now a fully editable object.

■ Quick tip

When you create files with plenty of trims and need to use them on a regular basis, save the file into the main symbol library, which will automatically open on start-up. Do this by saving the file under Application>Adobe Illustrator>Preset>Symbols. (For Windows users, locate the Adobe Illustrator folder and save it into the same Preset/symbol folder.)

Countless types of trim and design detail libraries can be created. Usually, when you start designing on Illustrator, you will have to gradually build the library up from scratch and then access your trims on the fly from your newly created library. Bear in mind, however, that it will take time to build up good content.

Trims and design details

The next part of this chapter looks at how best to design trims and design details. Countless design details and trims are available and this chapter will not be able to cover every single one of them. The focus will be on how to use Illustrator best to create trims and design details quickly and neatly.

When you design a trim or design detail from scratch, it is best to use a template image or freehand drawing. This will help you get the trim looking good faster. You have already created quite a few trims and design details in previous tutorials so, moving on from these, let's learn how to create more advanced trims and design details. Again, the collection of trims and details included in this tutorial is by no means exhaustive, it is more a foundation from which to build.

Zip puller

Zip pullers come in many different sizes, shapes and kinds. Every year, zip manufacturers will come up with new collections, containing new styles and shapes. The shape in this tutorial is a classic style; if you need to create more fancy zippers, the same design technique can be applied.

1 Start by designing half the zip puller's sliding part, either using a template or from scratch.

2 Mirror, duplicate and then join the sliding part.

3 For the puller, draw a rectangle that fits into the slider part.

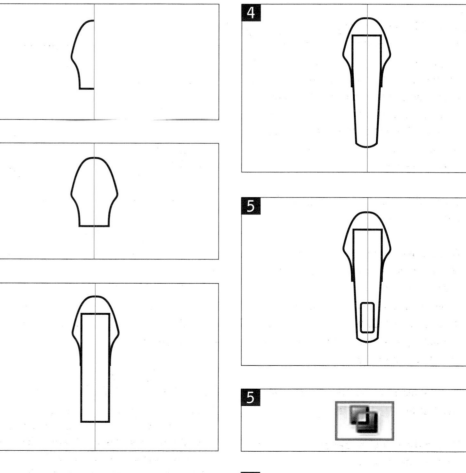

4 Transform the shape, using the Add Anchor Point tool and the white arrow (A).

5 Punch a hole through the puller, using a round corner rectangle shape and the Pathfinder palette's shape mode. Exclude overlapping areas.

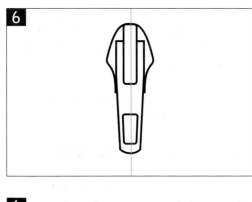

6 Finish by drawing a rounded rectangle shape for the puller's holding part.

7 Select all parts of the zip puller and use the Align palette to align them on a vertical axis. Group all the parts.

Buttons and metal bits (rivets, studs and so on)

You have already created a basic four-hole button design and rivets in previous tutorials. Metal bits are usually easy to represent, so you can design them quite quickly, as follows:

Pyramid stud

8 Draw a square.

9 Use the Knife tool to slice the square twice at 45-degree angles.

10 Fill in every quarter with different shades of grey to represent the pyramid's volume.

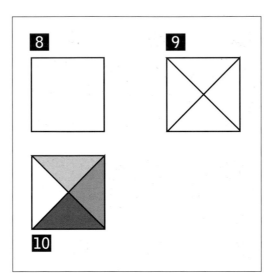

Pyramid stud

11 Group the four quarters.

Eyelets and snap button

12 Draw two circles.

13 Align them on both axes, using the align palette.

14 Select them both and, in the Pathfinder palette, under the shape mode, select Exclude Overlapping Shape Area and then press Expand.

15 Fill the new shape with white.

Your eyelet is ready. You can now copy it and use it for the snap stud design:

16 Add a couple of circles.

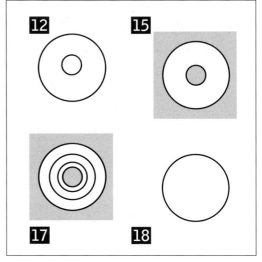

Eyelet and snaps

17 Align them on both axes, using the align palette.

18 Draw another circle for the other side of the snap stud.

Hook and eye

Eye:

19 Draw two circles, a big and a smaller one, as shown.

20 Using the Scissors tool, cut off unwanted segments.

21 Join the two circles.

22 Mirror the two circles and join the end anchor points.

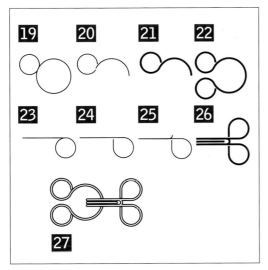

Hook and eye

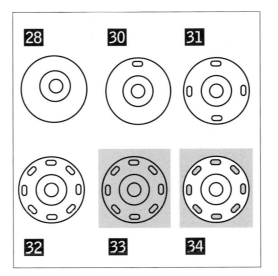

Sew-on snap fastener

Hook:

 23 Draw a circle and a straight line.

24 Cut off the top-left circle segment and in its place draw a straight line.

25 Add the central hook segment and curve, mirroring all the bits created for the hook.

26 Join at end anchor points.

27 Finish by outlining both the hook and the eye.

Sew-on snap fastener

28 Draw three circles.

29 Align them on both axes, using the align palette.

30 Draw a round-cornered rectangle on the inner edge of the biggest circle.

31 Using the centre of the circle as a target, rotate your round-cornered rectangle. Constrain it to 90 degrees and duplicate it. Do this three times.

32 Select the four rounded rectangles and rotate and duplicate them again, constraining them to a 45-degree angle as before.

33 Select all the rounded rectangles and group them.

34 Select the biggest circle and the rounded rectangles. In the Pathfinder palette, under the shape mode, press on the Exclude Overlapping Shape Area and then press Expand. Fill the shape with white.

35 Group all the components of the snap fastener.

Buckles, clips and toggles

Some buckles are quite simple and some sportswear clips can be very complex to draw. Here is a just small selection of buckles, clips and toggles.

Belt buckle

36 Draw a round-cornered rectangle, with a small value for the rounded corners.

37 Draw a second smaller one and align them both on the vertical axis only.

38 Apply a white fill to both rectangles.

39 With both rectangles selected, in the Pathfinder palette, under the Shape Mode, press on Subtract from Shape Area and then press expand.

40 Draw a vertical rectangle, going from the top to the bottom of the buckle on the left side.

41 Draw a straight horizontal segment with the Pen tool; apply a big stroke value and rounded caps.

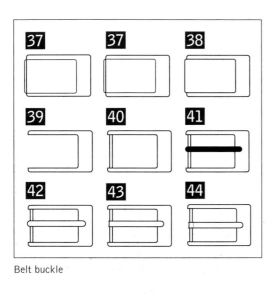

Belt buckle

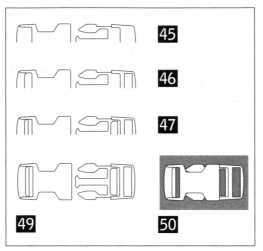

Plastic clip

Drawstring toggle

 Outline stroke the segment and apply a white fill and black outline.

 Transform the left end of the segment for a more realistic look.

44 Add detailing if required.

Plastic clips

45 Trace two half-clip outline shapes, one for each component.

46 Add details inside the shapes.

47 Mirror both components.

48 Join all the end anchor points.

49 Finish by using Subtract from Shape Area in the Pathfinder palette and then press Expand.

50 Close the clip to check the fitting.

Drawstring toggles

51 Trace half the toggle's outline shape (the outline stroke technique is very useful for this toggle's top part).

52 Add details inside the shapes.

53 Mirror and duplicate the toggle.

54 Join all the end anchor points.

55 Use Subtract from Shape Area in the Pathfinder palette and Add to Shape Area for different parts of the toggle (see picture). Press Expand.

56 To finish the trim, draw a string in two parts, going through the toggle.

■ Quick tip

When you design trims, using the pathfinder palette to subtract or exclude one shape from another, it is advisable that you check the final result by drawing a coloured rectangle behind the trim. This will help you to see if the shape has been excluded or subtracted properly.

subtracted shapes

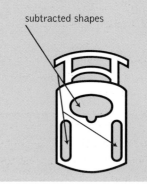

Decorative trims

Womenswear design uses countless types of decorative trim, such as crystals, beads and sequins. These trims are quite often simple in shape, but they tend to be used in great numbers over a garment, so we will look at how to make it possible to do this in a fast and relatively easy way. The other emphasis will be on the rendering of the reflective and shine effects that are often found with these kinds of trim.

Crystals and sequins

Crystals

Crystals have many different shapes, but they tend to be always symmetrical. To give a more glamorous and fun factor to your work, sparkle can be added to the crystals.

This is how to create crystals with a sparkly effect:

1 Start with a simple circle.

2 Shrink and duplicate it.

3 Create two guide lines on the vertical and horizontal axes of the centre of each circle.

4 In each circle, draw an octagon in the centre, using the Polygon tool.

5 Draw a segment going from the edge of the circle to the corner of the octagon, as shown.

6 Rotate and duplicate the segment, using the centre point of the circle as a target. Duplicate and constrain to a 45-degree angle.

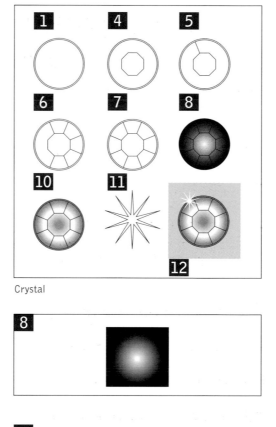

Crystal

7 Repeat this six times.

8 Select the outermost circle and fill it with the radial gradient colour found in the swatch palette.

9 In the Gradient palette (Menu> Window>Gradient) select the More Options pop-up menu on the top-right corner. You can then drag and drop solid colours into the gradient slider bar. If you drop a colour in the slide bar directly, this will create a new colour; if you drop it on the slider markers, this will replace the existing colour.

10 Move the sliders, if necessary, to match the gradient with the crystal.

11 To create the sparkle effect, use the Star tool, single clicking on

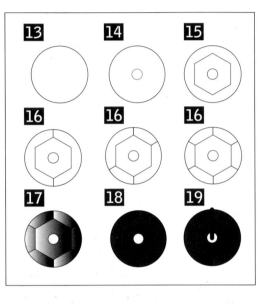

11

Star

Options

Radius 1: 6 mm

Radius 2: 1 mm

Points: 10

OK

Cancel

the art board to get the Star tool dialog box. Input a big value for radius one and a small value for radius two; input a fair amount of star points.

12 Apply a white fill to the star and resize it if necessary. Finish by placing it on the crystal (see page 149).

Sequins

Sequins are usually laid over a garment in blocks or to create an artwork. Sequins tend to be clustered, but rather than draw them one by one you can use Illustrator's Symbol Sprayer tool. The Symbol palette has already been used to create a trim library, but for individual trims we did not need to use the Sprayer tool. Once sprayed, symbols can be easily moved, resized, shifted, rotated and scrunched with related symbol tools.

First, you need to draw the sequin, which is achieved in a similar way to the crystal you just designed. This time, though, a more sophisticated way of rendering the shine of the

different facets will be used, by making each facet an individual object with its own gradient. **You can draw a sequin as follows:**

13 Draw two circles: a big one and a much smaller one. Copy the smaller circle.

14 Select them both and use the Pathfinder palette's Subtract from Shape Area. Press the Expand button.

15 Draw a hexagon and place it centrally between the circles. Paste the small circle in front. Select the small circle and the hexagon and repeat the same pathfinder operation as with both circles (see step 14).

16 Select the big circle and use the Knife tool to slice it in three parts: vertical, 45 degrees left and 45 degrees right. The lines should intersect the hexagon points. If you have difficulty doing this precisely, first draw a segment with the Pen tool where the cut line should be and then transform it into a guide (Command+5). You can then use this guide for your cutting.

17 Select the hexagon and fill it with a linear gradient, modifying the gradient to suit your needs, just as you did with the crystal.

21

18 Drop the new gradient in all the sequin facets. You can then change the angle of the gradient, in the Gradient palette, to follow the facets.

19 Finish the sequin by adding a stitch line, as shown.

To use the sequin with the Symbol Sprayer tool, do as follows:

20 Select the entire sequin and drop it in the Symbol palette.

21 Double click on the Symbol Sprayer tool. In the Symbolism Tools Options

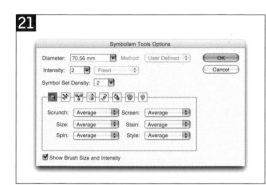

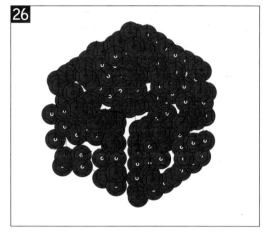

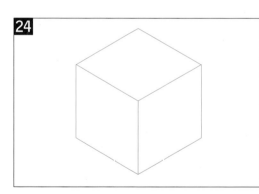

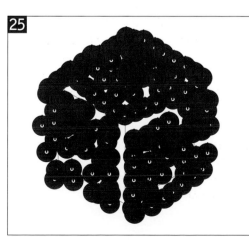

window, input a low (1–2) Symbol Set Density value. Press OK.

22 Spray the symbol on your art board by gently pressing and dragging the mouse.

23 If the density is too high or low, double click on the Sprayer tool again and use the density slide bar to change the value; you will see your sequins gathering or spreading accordingly.

24 When you have the desired density, draw a shape to use as a template for the object you want to produce in sequin – a cube, for example.

25 Spray over the template, making sure you fill all the gaps; don't worry if you spill over.

26 To get a less linear look and feel, spin your symbols, using the Symbol Spinner tool.

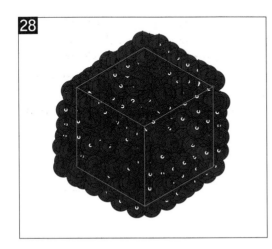

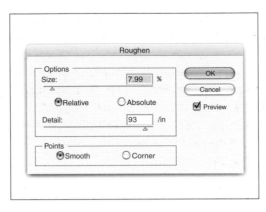

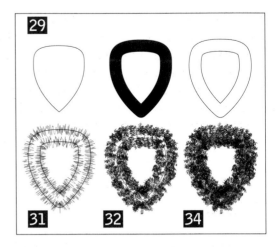

27 If there are still gaps between your symbols, use the Symbol Shifter tool.

28 To get rid of any unwanted symbols, expand the symbols (Menu>Object>Expand) and then ungroup and delete them individually.

You can also drop single symbols onto your artwork, just like you do with trim libraries.

Fur trimmings

It is time-intensive to reproduce fur manually. To get around this, you can use Illustrator's filters to great effect. This will give a convincing look and feel to fur trimmings in no time.

29 Draw a shape, which will become a fur trimming.

30 Copy and paste it in front.

31 Go to Menu>Filter>Distort>Roughen. Tick on the preview box and then play around with the details and size sliders to get the ideal look and feel.

32 Give the fur a thin stroke line, below 1pt. Lock the fur you just created and select the shape you made the fur with. Scale it so that it fits into the fur gap between the outer and inner fur path.

33 Transform the scaled object into fur with the roughen filter.

34 Your can repeat the last two steps several times until you have a fur trim that looks realistic.

Chapter 17
Creating Design Details with the Paintbrush

Illustrator's paintbrush is a versatile and very useful tool. You have already worked with artistic paintbrushes in chapter 15 to create wash effects. Artistic paintbrushes are the closest embodiment of a real brush. To create design details, we will use the pattern brush. Pattern brushes use up to five different components, which are called tiles, just like swatch patterns tiles. Pattern brushes, however, use the tile content to represent different areas of the brush stroke such as the side, inner corner, outer corner, start and end of a brush stroke.

When you paint with a pattern brush, the segment you create contains the source tile pattern repeating itself over the length of the segment. Creating tile patterns for a paintbrush is very similar to pattern swatches. Pattern brushes are the perfect tool with which to create design details, such as complex topstitching, ribbing, drawstrings, straps, webbings and so on. Let's start the tutorial with a simple rib pattern brush, using only the side tile.

Ribbing

In chapter 11, we created a simple rib for the T-shirt, making it from a segment with a thick dashed stroke line. There are some limitations to this technique: when the ribbing shape has non-perpendicular edges, for example, the ribbing can spill out of the shape. You cannot then expand the stroke lines to retouch the ribs individually, as you can with pattern brushes. The pattern brush can also be made into intricate ribbing details, going far beyond the simple dashed stroke line.

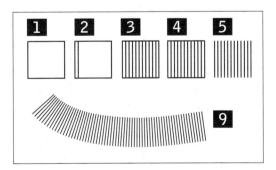

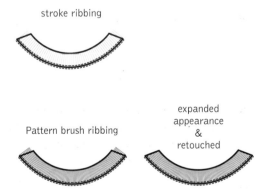

stroke ribbing

Pattern brush ribbing

expanded appearance & retouched

Let's start by creating the pattern brush side tile:

1 Draw a square and, using the white arrow, select one vertical segment; copy and paste it in front.

2 Move the pasted segment inside the square; constrain and duplicate it. To duplicate your move, press Command+D (or Control+D for Windows) as many times as are needed until the segments cover the square area.

3 Lock the square (Command+2); select the last segment and nudge it so that it is positioned just above the square vertical edge.

4 Select all the segments, in the Align palette, under Distribute Spacing, click on the Horizontal Distribute Space icon.

5 Unlock the square, giving it no stroke and fill.

6 Select and drag the square and all the segments, minus the last one, into the Brush palette.

7 In the New brush dialog box, select New Pattern Brush. Press OK.

7

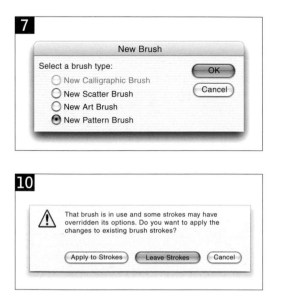

10

> ⚠ That brush is in use and some strokes may have overridden its options. Do you want to apply the changes to existing brush strokes?
>
> (Apply to Strokes)   (Leave Strokes)   (Cancel)

8 For now, simply press OK in the brush option window.

9 Pick the Brush tool in the Tool palette and use it to paint a long curved segment.

10 To change the width of the rib, double click on the brush pattern icon in the Brush palette. Tick the preview box and change the percentage value under Scale. Press OK. In the Warning dialog box press Apply to Strokes.

Pattern Brush Options

Name: [Pattern Brush 3]   (OK)
(Cancel)

None
Original
Azure Rings
Camouflage
Honeycomb
Jungle Stripes
Mediterranean Tiles
Pyramids

Size
Scale: [100%]
Spacing: [0%]

Flip
☐ Flip Along
☐ Flip Across

Colorization
Method: [None]
Key Color: [🖋 ■] (Tips)

Fit
◉ Stretch to fit
○ Add space to fit
○ Approximate path

■ **Quick tip**

You can apply a **pattern brush to any object or segment created on your art board**: simply select it and click on the pattern brush of your choice.

Topstitching

Pattern brushes can deal with complex designs such as, for example, flatlock topstitching. Only the default side tile is needed to create the topstitch. Let's start by drawing the topstitch pattern tile:

11 Draw the repeat sequence of a topstitch, using the pen tool.

12 Use vertical and horizontal guides to align the components.

13 Apply a dashed stroke on the stitching components.

14 Select all the topstitch components and drop them in the Brush palette. Select New Pattern Brush and press OK in the pattern brush option window.

15 Use the Brush tool to paint a segment or apply the pattern brush onto an existing segment.

■ **Quick tip**

You can change the size of your pattern brush by changing the stroke weight amount in the Stroke palette. This is much faster than using the pattern brush option window.

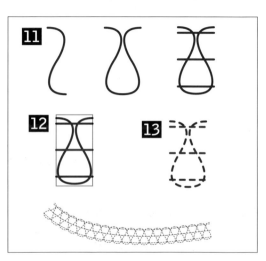

New Brush window detail (box 7):

Select a brush type:
○ New Calligraphic Brush
○ New Scatter Brush
○ New Art Brush
◉ New Pattern Brush
(OK) (Cancel)

To create a more realistic-looking topstitch, use the Pattern Brush tool to replace the dashed-stroke technique. Here are examples of pattern brush topstitch effects, created using the same technique as for flatlock stitching. You can also give a more realistic look to buttonholes by using brushes, rather than the zigzag filter, which applies a fixed amount of zigzag between anchor points. This gives an uneven look when the anchor points are not equidistant from each other.

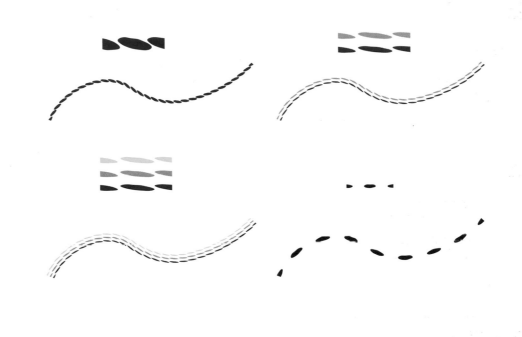

Zigzag

pattern brush

Drawstrings, straps and tapes

As explained in the chapter introduction, brushes can have up to five different tile components. In this tutorial, you will create pattern brushes with various combinations of tiles. Let's begin with a three-tile combination for a drawstring pattern brush.

Draw the side tile of the drawstring as follows:

1 Start by drawing a single component of your string.

2 Move it to the right; copy and constrain it. Press Command+D to repeat the move three times.

3 Find an anchor point on the repeat sequence as a marker onto which you will place a vertical guide; do the same for the other side.

4 Use the Knife tool to cut the unwanted part of the repeat sequence, using the guides for more precision.

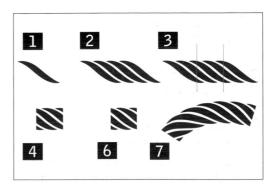

5 With the white arrow, select one anchor point on the left edge and another on the right edge with which it will connect. Average them on the horizontal axis. Repeat for all anchor points on both edges.

6 Select all the anchor points on the left edge and average them on the vertical axis. Repeat for the right edge.

7 Drop your artwork into the Brush palette and select pattern brush. Check the brush for any gaps or flaws by drawing a short curved segment.

Draw the endings of the drawstring as follows:

8 To make sure the endings will connect with the side tile, drag a horizontal guide in the middle of the side.

9 Draw the drawstring's right ending, making sure it is aligned with the side tile, as shown.

10 Select the drawstring's right ending and drag it into the pattern brush that is furthest to the right of the tile well, while pressing Alt (same for Windows). In the pattern brush option window, check that your drawstring ending appears. Press OK. Repeat same operation for the left drawstring ending, but drop it into the tile next to it.

9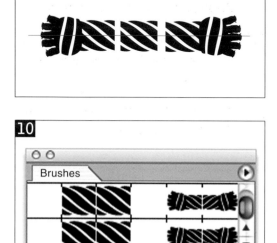

10

11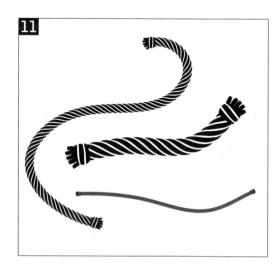

11 Test your brush and alter if necessary. You can also make the drawstring thinner by giving it a smaller stroke weight.

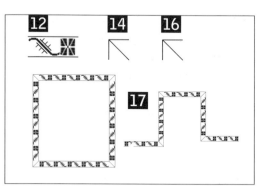

Decorative tapes

Using pattern brushes and the inner and outer corner tiles, you can also create decorative tapes. Tapes do not usually stretch, so you should not draw them with the freehand paintbrush, but apply them on rectangular objects or any other paths with 90-degree angles.

12 Start by drawing the side tile object (note how the embroidered tape effect is rendered by using simple ellipse shapes).

13 Drop the object into the Brush palette and select pattern brush.

14 Create the outer corner tile object, representing how a flat tape would look when applied onto a corner. (To save time, avoid complicated corner designs; keep it simple.)

15 Drag the corner object into the pattern brush that is furthest to the left of the tile well, while pressing Alt (same for Windows).

16 Create the inner corner tile, which in this case is the same as the outer corner one. Alt drag it into the fourth well from the left.

17 Create a shape, using 90-degree angles.

Straps

Straps can be applied using the Brush tool and created with the pattern brush. Straps are created in a similar way to drawstrings.

18 Create a side tile and drop it into the Brush palette, select pattern brush.

19 Draw the right end tile and drop it into the palette that is furthest to the right of the well.

20 Draw the left end tile and drop it into the well next to the right end tile.

21 You can now draw your strap either with the Paintbrush tool or apply it onto any chosen segment.

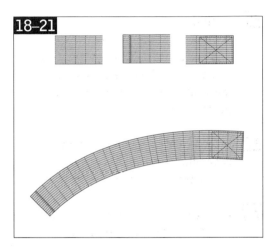

Elasticated waists, ruching and folds

The pattern brush is not only useful for design details but also for entire parts of a garment. You could, in theory, paint trousers in two brush strokes simply by using individual pattern brush tiles as different components for a trouser leg. The pattern brush is very useful for parts of garments that require lots of anchor points and fine detailing, such as elasticated waists, ruching or folds on hem lines.

Hem folds

1 To give your hem fold a more realistic look, draw it freehand and scan it in. Place the scanned file as a template onto your Illustrator document. Trace the fold sequence manually with the Pen tool.

2 Mirror the fold and check that it will repeat itself flawlessly.

3 Drop the hem fold shape into the Brush palette. Select New Pattern Brush.

4 Create the left ending of the pattern brush, in this case a simple corner segment. Make sure that your left end segment is horizontally aligned with the side tile; if not, they will not match (see picture).

5 Alt drop your segment into the tile positioned before the right end one.

6 Draw the right end tile (in this case, simply mirror the left end tile) and Alt drop it in to the tile that is furthest to the right.

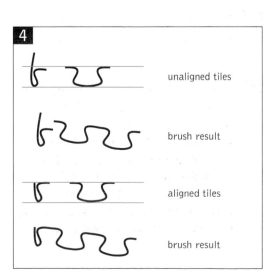

unaligned tiles

brush result

aligned tiles

brush result

7   Use the paintbrush to draw a curved line to check for any gaps or problems with the pattern brush.

You can easily retouch your brush by scaling the tile elements on your art board and Alt dropping them back over the old ones in the Brush palette. Once you have painted a segment with the paintbrush tool on the art board, you can easily alter it with the white arrow, just as you would alter any other segment.

To give the hem fold a more flowing and less rigid look, use the Roughen filter, making the brush stroke 0.5pt thick in order to have more folds per segment.

To join painted fold segments with your garment, simply expand its appearance (Menu>Object>Expand Appearance). Average and then join the pattern brush and garment end anchor points together.

To create pleats matching the folds, create a new pattern brush, using the hem fold pattern brush components, to which you will add pleat lines.

Using the Roughen filter

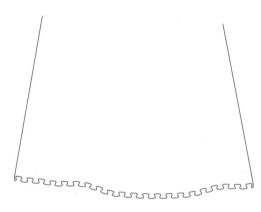

Joining the painted segment to garment

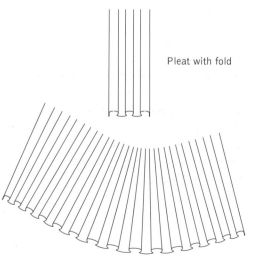

Pleat with fold

Ruching and ruffling

Ruching and ruffles can be easily created with a pattern brush, by means of a similar technique to that used for hem folds. Ruches and ruffles tend to be more random than folds, so you will need to create the brush accordingly. A good trick is to draw a longer tile segment, which allows for more random components within it. For a more natural effect, draw a ruche or ruffle freehand and then place it as a template in Illustrator. Trace it and use as your new pattern brush.

8   Draw the side tile, either using a freehand template or drawing directly with the Pen tool.

9   Select all the top anchor points and average them horizontally. Draw a straight line.

10   Drop two guide lines on each side of your ruffle. Add an anchor point that is furthest to the left of the ruffle, where it intersects with the guide line. Move and duplicate it on the right side of the ruffle. Get rid of the unwanted segments.

11   Select all the anchor points on the left edge; average them vertically and repeat the process for the right side.

12   Drag your artwork into the brush palette and select pattern brush.

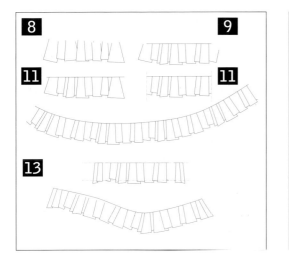

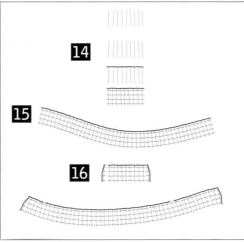

13 Draw the left and right end tiles. Alt drag and drop them in the brush palette in the corresponding tile wells. Make sure that the left and right end tiles are centred with your side tile (use a guide line to help you).

As with the hem fold, you can retouch, expand the appearance and join your ruffle to any garment shape.

Elasticated waist and cuffs

An elasticated waist and cuffs are created using the same technique as for the folds and ruffles. Elasticated hems and cuffs usually contain topstitching, random fold lines and a hem.

14 Draw a side tile using the same technique as with the ruffle and hem fold, make sure that your left edge will match with the right one. To achieve

credible random lines, use the Roughen filter.

15 Drop into the Brush palette, select pattern brush. Try the brush out.

16 Add left and right end tiles to finish the pattern brush.

There are endless design possibilities for the details and entire parts of garments that can be created with pattern brushes and I hope these examples will inspire you to design many new brushes. Remember that you should save your brushes in a dedicated file that can then be accessed at any time and used on any garments design (see Trim Libraries, Chapter 16).

Chapter 18
Trim Branding and Fashion Graphics

Many fashion companies rely heavily on graphic design to market their products. The increase over the past 25 years in logos, trim branding, labelling, packaging and prints artwork on and around garments has been phenomenal. The advent of computers and digital media technology, coupled with faster, better and cheaper production means, has been a key factor in this growth. From the very beginning, Illustrator was created primarily for graphic designers and it has evolved into a high-end professional graphic application. This chapter will cover the various aspects of graphic design for fashion, such as logotype graphic styles and trim branding. The usual set-up in a fashion company is to have a graphic designer in charge of producing logos and prints for garments, usually under the art direction of a fashion designer. Bearing this in mind, this chapter takes just a glancing look at various features covering logo design and trim branding and is therefore far from exhaustive.

Creating a logo

A logotype is a stylized written display of a brand name, produced on any label, trim or garment. You have already learned in the basic tutorials how to type text, but stopped short of transforming any typeface into editable paths and anchor points. When you type text in Illustrator, the text appears just as it does on a word processing or email application. You can highlight and edit words at any time, but you are limited to the typefaces installed on your system. You can stretch and rotate text with the black arrow and the bounding box, but not much more. If you want to create a unique brand-name logo, you can draw it by hand, scan it and trace it or directly use the Type tool in Illustrator. In this tutorial, you will create a logo, using the Type tool and a system typeface:

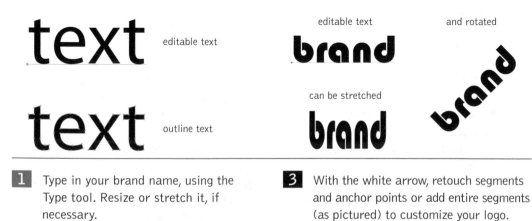

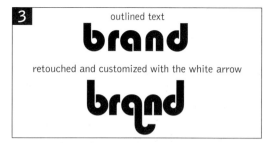

Customized logo from system typeface

1 Type in your brand name, using the Type tool. Resize or stretch it, if necessary.

2 Go to Menu>Type>Create Outlines (or Command+Shift+O).

3 With the white arrow, retouch segments and anchor points or add entire segments (as pictured) to customize your logo.

4 When your logo is ready, you should group it.

This is the simplest way to create a logo, but Illustrator's Graphic Styles (called Style in Illustrator 10) feature can help you go much further.

Working with Graphic Styles

Illustrator's Graphic Styles is a style set with a distinctive graphic look. When you apply a graphic style to your logo or object, it will not change the logo's path structure; you can at any time revert to your original logo. You can use Illustrator's pre-designed graphic styles or create your own.

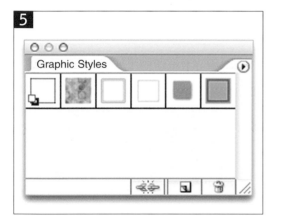

using Illustrator preset graphic style

preset graphic style customized with the Appearance palette

Start by applying a pre-designed graphic style to your logo:

5 Make sure the Graphic Styles and Appearance palettes are visible.

6 Select your logo. In the Appearance palette you should see a black fill and no stroke attribute (or any other representation of your logo fill and stroke combination).

7 In the Graphic Styles palette, select any swatch by single clicking on it.

The selected graphic style might not look right for your logo. You can easily **customize a graphic style** to suit your artwork:

8 Using the black arrow, select the logo on which you applied a preset graphic style.

9 In the Appearance palette, single click on the fill or stroke attribute to select it.

10 You can now alter the graphic style attributes by changing the stroke weight, colour and dash in related palettes.

11 When you have finished customizing the style, press and drag its icon (top left) from the Appearance palette to the Style palette, to save the changes.

You can also add new attributes and effects to a graphic style.

To add an attribute to a graphic style, do the following:

12 Select your logo with the new customized graphic style. In the Appearance palette, click on the palette pop-up option menu (top right) then select Add New Stroke.

13 The new stroke attribute will stack on top of the previous ones. You can change stacking order of the attributes in the appearance palette by dragging them above or below one another.

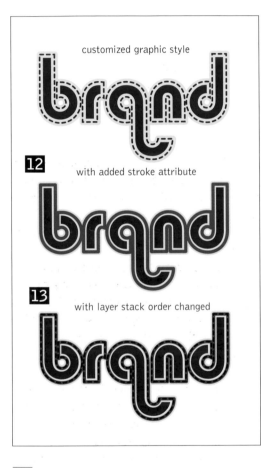

customized graphic style

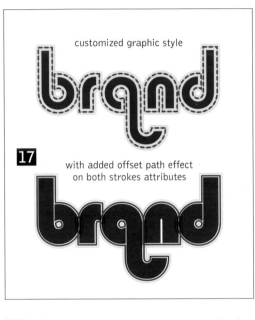

customized graphic style

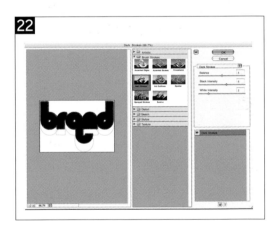

12 with added stroke attribute

13 with layer stack order changed

17 with added offset path effect
on both strokes attributes

14 Alter the new stroke attribute in related palettes.

To add an effect to graphic styles attributes, do the following:

15 Select your logo. In the Appearance palette, select the attribute onto which you want to add an effect.

16 Go to Menu>Effect>Path>Offset Path (for example).

17 In the offset path dialog box, tick on Preview and change the offset value to suit your logo. Press OK.

18 You might need to alter the attributes in related palettes to make the effect look better on your logo.

You can **add more realistic effects to radically alter your logo** by using Photoshop Effects, located in the Effect menu below Photoshop Effects.

Before using any Photoshop effects, you should first rasterize your logo or object. Rasterizing is the process of transforming any vector graphic object into a bitmap (pixel) image.

To use Photoshop effects on your entire logo, do the following:

19 Go to Menu>File>Document Color Setup>RGB colour.

20 Select your latest logo with a graphic style.

21 Go to Menu>Object>Rasterize. In the Rasterize dialog box, select a resolution of 300dpi and leave the rest untouched. Press OK.

22 Go to (for example)

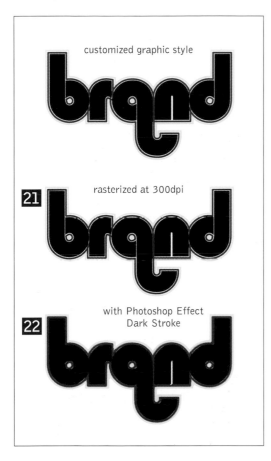

customized graphic style

21 rasterized at 300dpi

22 with Photoshop Effect
Dark Stroke

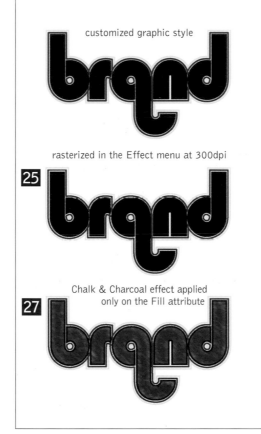

customized graphic style

25 rasterized in the Effect menu at 300dpi

27 Chalk & Charcoal effect applied
only on the Fill attribute

Default style icon

Menu>Effect>Brush Strokes>Dark
Strokes. Adjust the settings to get the
look you want. Press OK.

**You can also add Photoshop effects on your
logo's individual attributes directly:**

23 Go to Menu>File>Document Color
Setup>RGB colour.

24 Select your latest logo with a graphic
style.

25 Go to Menu>Effect>Rasterize. In the
Rasterize dialog box, select a
resolution of 300dpi and leave the rest
untouched. Press OK.

26 In the Appearance palette, select the
Fill attribute.

27 Go to (for example) Menu>Effect>
Blur>Sketch>Chalk&Charcoal. Adjust
the settings to get the look you want.
Press OK.

The advantage of using this technique is that
you can, at any time, alter, delete or add any
attributes you wish. On the other hand, when
you apply effects to your entire logo
(object), you cannot change anything once it
has been applied.

You can also **create your own graphic
style** from scratch simply by selecting an
object or logo without any style attribute. In
the Appearance palette, add a stroke or fill
attribute in the palette pop-up option menu.
Build up your own graphic style by adding
strokes and effects.

At any time, you can get rid of the graphic
style applied to your object by selecting the
default style in the style palette. You can
also expand a style appearance in
Menu>Object>Expand Appearance. This will
transform the style into editable paths and
anchor points. Note that you cannot do this
with a graphic styles attribute containing
Photoshop effects.

Trim branding

When your logo is ready, or your graphic design department provides you with the company logo, you can either apply it to your garment designs or create a branding library (see chapter 16) containing all the brand's different logos and labels types (flag, tag, inside label, patch and so on). Logos should not be distorted, so always remember to scale your logo proportionally (pressing Shift) to avoid stretching. You will sometimes need to write a brand name into a button and make it fit around the button edge. The simplest way to do this is to use Illustator's Path Type tool.

To create a logo along a path, do the following:

1 Create a button or take one from your trim library.

2 Select your outer-most circle and scale it down. Constrain and duplicate it as shown.

3 Select the Path Type tool and single click anywhere on the new circle.

4 Type in the brand name, using a typeface similar to that of the brand logo, if possible.

5 Using the white arrow, press and drag the vertical text input bar to the left of your logo. This will enable you to align your logo horizontally.

6 Copy paste in front the entire text path and then rotate it.

7 Add decorative elements, if necessary.

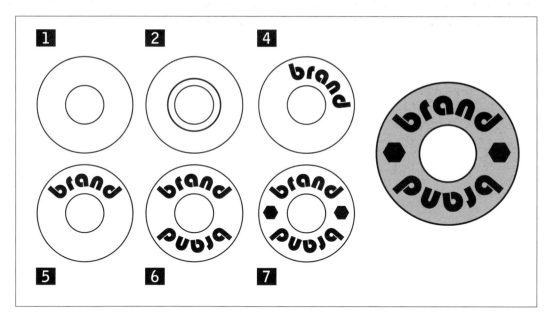

You can now drop your button into the Symbol palette to create the first element of a trim branding library.

This technique is limited to the use of ready-made typefaces and will not work with a customized logo. Read the next chapter to see how you can create a button branding with warp effects.

Chapter 19
Varying and Communicating Your Designs

One of the key change factors in today's fashion world is the ever-increasing number of garments and brands available on the market. Designers are expected to produce more and more styles, collections, speed editions, special editions and variations in less and less time. Illustrator can help the designer to **vary** his work in many ways, one being the use of the effect functions. Effect functions can dramatically alter your original shape in no time and therefore reduce the amount of time spent on creating new shapes and variations. When fashion designers work on a new collection, they usually start by presenting the range internally. The selected designs will then have to be sent to a factory or production agent for the prototyping and sampling process to start. At the same time, the designs might be presented to key clients as a preview for the coming collection. With this kind of set-up, if you choose to create only one flat drawing with a certain style you run the risk of your design not being well received or understood by some parties. For example, a designer with a rigid and simple style might work well with factories but might bore the buyers. So what is the solution? Create two or three versions of the same design? Clearly this can be counter-productive, unless of course a designer takes advantage of Illustrator's effect functions to alter the look and feel of the designs simply and swiftly and therefore better **communicate** them to different parties.

Using the Warp Effect Function

Warp effects are a fun and very fast way to quickly modify any garment shape into a new one.

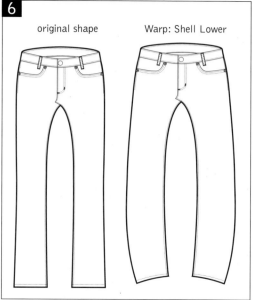

4

Warp Options

Style: Bulge

○ Horizontal   ● Vertical

OK

Cancel

☑ Preview

Bend: 10 %

Distortion

Horizontal: 0 %

Vertical: -5 %

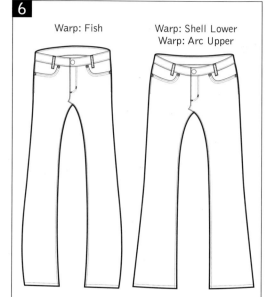

6

original shape   Warp: Shell Lower

6

Warp: Fish   Warp: Shell Lower
Warp: Arc Upper

To apply warp effects to your designs, do the following:

1 Open a flat drawing created in a previous tutorial, such as the jeans. Copy and paste it into a new document.

2 Select all the details and shape.

3 Go to Menu>Effect>Warp>Bulge (or any other).

4 In the warp option dialog box, tick Preview and move the slider bar to modify the effect strength and type. Press OK to confirm. Your underlying shape is not altered, so you can duplicate the shape to create another variation.

5 When your shape is copied, go to the Appearance palette, select the Warp instance and delete it by clicking on the bin icon. Your shape is back to normal.

6 Repeat steps 2 to 5 to create countless variations with different warp effects.

You can also **warp the logo** you created in chapter 18 to fit a button shape (using the Arc warp function). Note that this effect will distort your logo, which might not be suitable for the corporate ID.

Varying your design with the Mesh Envelop Distort

Mesh envelop enables you to have more control on the distortion effect by placing an editable mesh over your shape. This function has a drawback though: it is hard to keep any mesh envelop distortion symmetrical. It's therefore advisable to have a low-count mesh, to avoid complications.

3

Envelope Mesh

Mesh

Rows: 3

Columns: 3

OK

Cancel

Preview

4

5

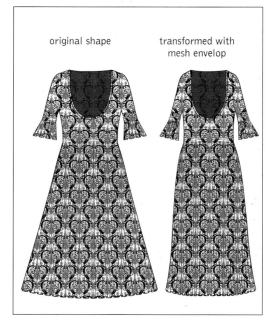

original shape   transformed with mesh envelop

To create a mesh envelop distort, do the following:

1 Open a shape created in previous tutorials. Copy paste it into a new document; group all the components.

2 Go to Menu>Object>Envelop Distort>Make with Mesh (or Command+Alt+M).

3 In the mesh option dialog box, input two for column and one for row. Press OK.

4 Select the Mesh tool in the Tool palette.

5 Go over your shape on the CF line at waistline height and single click. This will create a mesh row. Single click in different positions along the CF line to create more mesh rows.

6 Press and drag the mesh anchor points to alter the dress shape and details. Make sure you move the left and right anchor points in equal measures, to avoid asymmetrical results.

Using effects to alter a pattern brush

You can alter pattern brushes once they are applied to a segment or brush stroke with the **Free Distort Effect** (Menu>Effect>Distort&Transform>Free Distort).

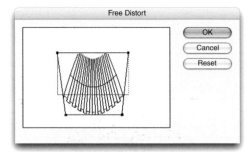

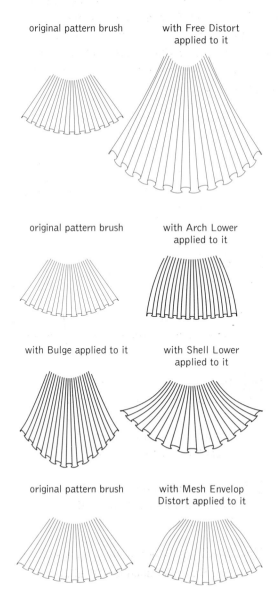

original pattern brush   with Free Distort applied to it

original pattern brush   with Arch Lower applied to it

with Bulge applied to it   with Shell Lower applied to it

original pattern brush   with Mesh Envelop Distort applied to it

control over the distortion. You can also use the **Envelope Distort, Make with Mesh:** Menu>Objects>Envelop Distort>Make with Mesh. (Command+Alt+M). This creates a mesh with which you can modulate the brush content, using the same technique as with a garment shape.

You can, for example, distort the folded hem brush so that it tapers in more dramatically to fit a dress shape. Free distort can be a bit limited, whereas **Envelop Distort** functions are much better suited to creating countless variations of pattern brushes. Select a segment with the pattern brush applied to it and go to Menu>Objects>Envelop Distort> Make with Wrap. (Command+Alt+W). In the dialog box, you can choose various predefined shapes onto which your pattern brush will fit. Tick the preview box for more

Creating a more organic and freehand look

All garment flats contained in the tutorials have been created to look as close as possible to an actual garment as regards cut and proportions. This kind of drawing is well suited for a manufacturer. Taking this as a starting point, you can modify and distort the flat to get a more freehand and organic look, using Illustrator's various distortion effects and tools. The resulting drawing will be suitable for a sales catalogue, as it will **communicate** the style and vibe of a collection. Your garment will look less rigid and have more edge.

Let's start by working with the **Liquify tools**, to get a freehand and uneven look. Liquify tools are easy and fun to use and can alter your original flat in no time:

1 Open a flat drawing created in a previous tutorial, such as the jacket. Copy and paste it into a new document.

2 On your flat drawing, select only the elements that will benefit from a distortion, such as the shape and topstitch. Do not select elements such as buttons.

3 In the Tool palette, tear off the Liquify tool floating palette.

4 Double click on the Warp tool (first left). In the Tool Option dialog box, under Warp Option, input a low detail amount and high simplicity amount. For now, leave the other options untouched. Press OK.

5 Press and drag the Warp tool over your jacket shape, from top to bottom, going along the edges. You can move slightly to the left or right to accentuate the distortion.

6 If the result is not satisfactory, modify the tool options or the brush size.

7 Try using other Liquify tools for specific areas, such as the elbows.

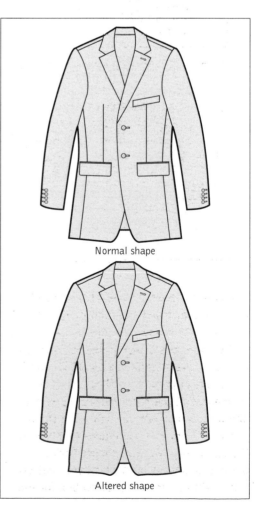

Normal shape

Altered shape

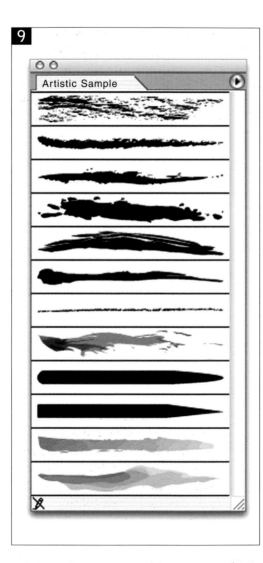

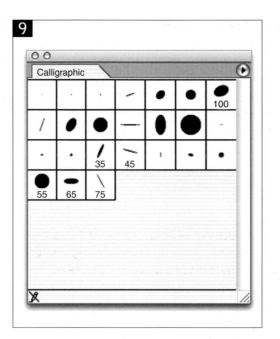

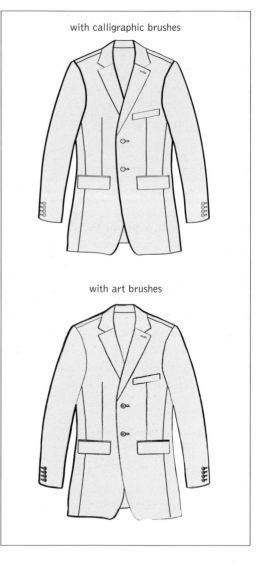

with calligraphic brushes

with art brushes

Be careful not to overdo the effects! Always use a low intensity to avoid unpleasant results. Note that the Liquify tools cannot be used on objects containing text or symbols.

After having loosened the jacket shape with the Liquify tools, you can apply some art brushes to give the design an even more organic and freehand look and feel.

To apply art brushes to your garment, do as follows:

8   Select the shape outline.

9   In the Brush palette, choose an art or calligraphic brush (you can open more art and calligraphic brushes if necessary).

10   Single click to select the brush to be applied to the shape.

11   Repeat with different brushes for different parts of your design (details, topstitch and so on).

You can modify or create your own brush to suit your style and needs (see chapter 17). Try to use a small stroke weight to avoid smudgy and undefined strokes.

Chapter 20
Sharing Your Design

This final chapter looks at how to best prepare Illustrator files to be shared with other parties, depending on the situation and their needs. Good communication is essential and preventing any technical issues is important if you want to avoid time wastage and complications. Quite often, factories or production agents do not work with Illustrator and will request your files in a shareable format, such as PDF. There are three types of communication scenarios covered in this chapter: firstly, sending your files by email; secondly, printing your files for paper presentations and, finally, preparing your files as content for page layout applications, such as Adobe Indesign or QuarkXpress. A good starting point is to talk to your correspondents and ask them exactly what kind of software and hardware they work with. The best strategy is to adapt to different situations and be as flexible as possible.

Sending your files by email

Email has been around for the last 10 years but only recently, with the advent of ADSL and Broadband, has email been able to handle large-file transfer. Even so, companies quite often cap their outgoing and incoming data size to avoid bottlenecks and unwanted file transfers. It is therefore important to ascertain the policy of your company and your correspondent on file transfer before sending huge files. The second step is to ask your correspondent whether they work with or own Adobe Acrobat Reader (assuming they do not own or work with Illustrator). Acrobat Reader is based on the PDF (Portable Document File) technology developed by Adobe. It is free to download from adobe.com and usually comes bundled with Mac OS X and Windows. Illustrator can automatically save files in PDF format.

There are a few things you should know and do before sending a PDF file:

 Open your Illustrator document that needs to be sent by email.

2 Make sure that there are no objects outside the A4 page (select all to check this, since you could have invisible stray points outside the page).

3 Select all your typefaces and outline them (this will make the file size much lighter).

4 In the Swatch, Brush, Style and Symbol palettes, choose Select All Unused in the option pop-up menu. Then single click the trashcan icon. This will make your file size lighter.

5 Save as (Command+Shift+S) your document in a new folder.

6 In the Save As Dialog box, under Format, select Adobe PDF and press OK (Illustrator 10). For version 12, select Illustrator default settings. More advanced options are available, but the default format works in 99 per cent of cases. Select a PDF version (check with your correspondent which version they use). Press OK to confirm.

■ Quick tip

Adobe Acrobat Reader is based on the A4 format (or US letter). Avoid sending files that are bigger than A4 format, such as original size graphic prints. Acrobat will automatically reduce any oversize format back to A4 size.

Preparing your files for paper presentation

Paper is usually the most natural way for a designer to communicate and present his/her work. There are a few things a designer should bear in mind when wanting to produce high quality and colour-accurate prints, as described below.

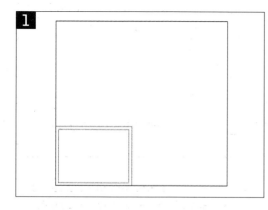

Page tiling

Assuming you have the right printer, you can print up to A3 format, but Illustrator can handle documents measuring up to three metres square. These kinds of large documents can be printed using the tiling method. Page tiling displays tiles of A4 or A3 pages over any given art board size. For example, an art board size of 63 x 60cm will require a tiling of six A4 pages. Page tiling is only useful if you create artworks to the actual size (for example, T-shirt graphic prints). You can print the artwork out as a mock-up to place on your T-shirt. To do this, do as follow **for Illustrator 10 and below only:**

1 Open a new document and input a document size that fits your artwork size: for example,

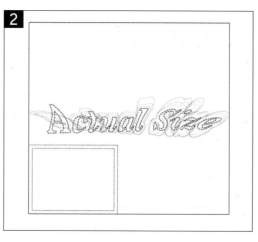

630 x 600mm. By default, Illustrator will place a single A4 page tile or your new document.

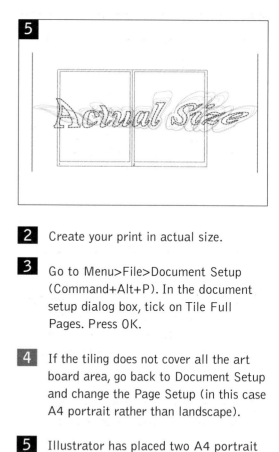

2 Create your print in actual size.

3 Go to Menu>File>Document Setup (Command+Alt+P). In the document setup dialog box, tick on Tile Full Pages. Press OK.

4 If the tiling does not cover all the art board area, go back to Document Setup and change the Page Setup (in this case A4 portrait rather than landscape).

5 Illustrator has placed two A4 portrait pages in the centre of the art board.

6 To change this, use the Page tool, which is embedded with the Hand tool. Simply press and drag one page to the lower left corner of your art board and then release.

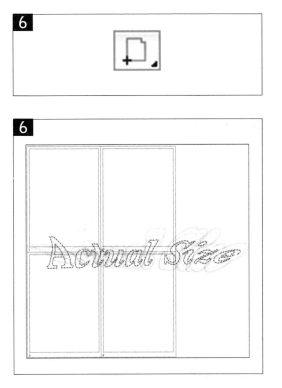

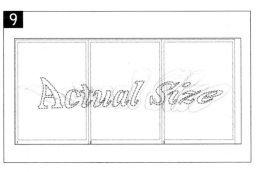

7 If the tiling still does not cover the art board (in this case widthwise), go again to Document Setup and change the document width to a greater value (in this case 650 mm).

8 Illustrator will automatically add more tiles to cover the art board.

9 Obviously, for this artwork we only need three A4 pages. Go back to the Document Setup and change the document height to 300mm. Illustrator will again automatically resize the art board and page tiling, as shown.

10 You can now print your artwork; press Command+P or go to Menu>File>Print. Note that you will have gaps between the pages if your printer does not handle full-page prints.

With Illustrator CS2, page tiling is much easier and faster to achieve:

1 Open a new document and input a document size that fits your artwork size: for example, 630 x 600mm. By

default, Illustrator will place a single A4 page tile on your new document.

2 Create your print in actual size.

3 Go to Menu>File>Print (or Command+P). In the dialog box, under the top-left box, select Setup. Then, under Crop Artwork, select Artwork Bounding Box. Below, under Tiling, select Tile Full Pages and, under Overlap, input a value equivalent to your printer's margins (5mm for example). You will see, in the lower left box, the page tiling updating itself automatically as you change the settings.

Multiple-page printout

Illustrator is not the best application to use when you want to print out many single A4 or A3 pages. Avoid having too many garment designs on one document. Refer to 'Preparing your files for page layout applications' to find out how to handle a print output for multiple single pages. The best way to work with Illustrator, when designing a collection, is to keep one file per garment style and print them one by one.

Colour management

The hardest thing about printing on paper is to match the screen colours with the ones on your print. Some people make their living out of managing colour from screen to paper. The difficulty lies in the fact that colours on your screen are RGB based and generated from light, whereas printers use CMYK inks to represent the same colours Working in CMYK colour mode on Illustrator should help you to get better results. Achieving a decent colour match is usually a question of trial and error.

A good way to work this out is to use physical Pantone colour cards or collection colour cards, from which you will create your colourways on screen. The next step is to print the digital colour card and match it with your original swatch. If a colour does not match, try to see whether it has too much yellow,

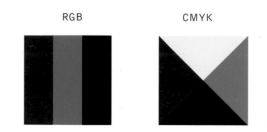

RGB   CMYK

cyan or magenta, or if it is too dark or light. You can then adjust the CMYK sliders on screen. Try to make several swatches per colouway, each with different CMYK values. Bear in mind that when you colour-manage with one printer, you may get totally different results with another and, most annoyingly, even the same printer might generate different results, depending on the ink supplied or ink level. Make sure that whatever you print out for clients is done well in advance and on the same printer as the one you colour-managed.

Preparing your files for page layout application

Illustrator handles one-page artwork well, but is not so good for multiple-page layout. In fact, there is no multiple-page mode in

Illustrator. The only way around this is to create a document with a big art board and tile multiple A4 pages, but this is cumbersome and leads to big file size, which will not transfer well to PDF file format. The best thing to do is to have only one garment flat drawing per A4 page. If you or your graphic team work with QuarkXpress, you will need to save a copy of your original file in EPS format (Encapsulated Post Script).

If you or your colleagues work with Adobe InDesign, you can also save your file in EPS format or as Illustrator format. You can also save them in PDF format for Adobe Acrobat (not Reader but full version), which can create a multiple-page PDF document. Quite often, bigger companies use database applications such as Quest PDM to manage, print and distribute a collection over networks. Depending on the application your company uses, you can either save your file in EPS or PDF. It's common sense to ask the IT department and ascertain the best format to use.

A LAST WORD

This is it. You have completed the entire tutorial. Congratulations! I hope you have enjoyed it and that it will help you become more prolific and creative when working on your next collection. If there is one last piece of advice, it can only be that you should keep on practising what you have just learned because, unfortunately, without practice all this can be forgotten only too quickly!

Kevin Tallon

Index